The Secret Life of CATS

By Arline Bleecker
Cover illustration by Peter Warner

Contents

THE CATS IN OUR LIVES...

I know I don't have to sell you on cats. They grab our attention – and our hearts – and we never want to let them go. We know that all it takes is one look at that regal body, one contented purr or the way they wrap their sleek bodies around our ankles, and we stop whatever we are doing to focus on them.

And they expect nothing less.

That's how it's been for me ever since Kitty companion *numero uno* entered my life 17 years ago...followed by a never-ending parade of cats. How typical. So much in life comes and goes, but our cats just seem to keep coming. Stray cats have an uncanny knack for showing up – unannounced – on my doorstep, in a parking lot, or peering out at me from beneath bushes. It's as if a newsletter circulates in the cat world that says "Pssst. A good and loving home," with my address on it.

That's how most of my cats acquired me, and I've adored every one.

Currently residing with me and my husband are Red, Blueberry, Little Guy and Kitten. (As you can tell, I'm not very creative about names, mainly because it never matters much what I name them. They never come when called anyway.)

Little Guy is a plume-tailed, toffee-colored long-hair whose amber eyes peered out at me from a clump of ferns one afternoon a few years ago. Now, he smugly reigns as Top Cat in our household.

Our most recent addition is Kitten, a nervous pint-sized, mottled female whose coloring gives her the appearance of two cats – depending on which end you're looking at.

On her front half, her coat is tortoiseshell; her back end is pure Russian Blue. And with her continually startled expression, she's as funny-looking as she is charming. British poet Robert Southey wrote: "A kitten is in the animal world what a rosebud is in the garden."

Our little Kitten lives up to the name, symbolic of sweet promise and full of life.

The oldest cats sharing our household are Blueberry, a chubby calico, and Red, a carrot-colored tabby – ages 15 and 14 respectively. In comparison to the energy and playfulness of the younger two Kitties, the light glitters in these cats' eyes a bit more faintly now. But they are still wonderful creatures, nonetheless.

For beauty's sake alone, any cat is a joy to observe. Talking about his own cats' amazing grace, the choreographer George Balanchine once remarked: "At last I have a body worth choreographing for." (And Balanchine didn't even have to teach them how to do a pirouette!)

A cat's amazing flexibility comes courtesy of a extraordinarily flexible spine – bringing to mind an elasticity described by 19th-century physicist John Tyndall as only one-tenth less than that of India rubber.

In fact, just about every feature of their anatomy suits them perfectly – and adds to our cat-watching pleasure. They're like acrobats in fur coats (or more accurately, acro-*cats*); elusive hunters with some of the keenest senses in the animal kingdom. And though they don't stand very tall, they can stretch their bodies as long as is needed.

We fix our gaze on our cats' mysterious eyes, as big as marbles and the colors of jewels. Their sweet round faces, and toasty-warm bodies are just the right size for cuddling. And . . . they *purr*!

We are cat addicts, indeed. The 60 million of us who share our lives with them have come to rely on our cats for the support of our souls.

It has probably always been that way.

They are regal, snooty and divine. It's a small wonder that the Egyptians worshiped them. Even now, there are times when I swear I can hear mine saying, "Your ancestors were crawling around in caves while mine were being idolized. So hurry up with that can opener!"

In fact, I never can quite decide if I have cats or if they have me. When I lived with as many as seven of them, food-buying was a chore indeed. One day, I decided to purchase 16 cases of cat chow at once. "She must be mad!" I heard the cashier mumble to a co-worker.

I recall the first time I was asked by a total stranger: "Do you have cats, ma'am?"

"How can you tell?" I replied, surprised by his insight.

"Look at your shirt," he said. It was covered with cat hair.

Without doubt, their evidence is everywhere. And I wear it proudly.

As a writer, being at home among them all the time gives me a great deal of pleasure. Their limber little bodies are everywhere – draped over the back of a chair, under the sofa cushions – creating small landscapes of leisure and loveliness.

But I also can tell you that it would be easier to write with a herd of elephants in my room than a single cat.

They walk on my computer keyboard, camp out on top of my books, make nests in my notes, gladly wreck my research, nibble on the end of my pencil, or insist I drop everything altogether to scratch an ear or two. And if they don't like what I write ... they just shred it to pieces. (They loved it when I was working on this book. After all, it's all about them!)

Even if you're living with just one cat, you know by now that she has as many personalities as she has proverbial lives. Well, maybe not nine, but darn close. Enough, at least, to keep you forever wondering "Who is this cat?"

In the final analysis, their mysterious world may indeed be known only to them. But who could fault us for trying to figure them out? Not only is it fun to probe their mysteries, but the more we find out about them, the more it stirs our curiosity.

I hope this book brings you new insights – some funny, some useful – to help you better understand the secret life of your cat.

If you've got unusual cats or a great cat tale, write and tell us about them. Maybe we'll use the best of them in our next book!

FELINE
PHILOSOPHY

"I had been told that the training procedure with cats was difficult. It's not. Mine had me trained in two days."
–*Comedian Bill Dana*

Cats have been associating with humans for about five million years, only half as long as domesticated dogs have.

That's why we cat lovers always say our cats still have one paw in the jungle. From the standpoint of evolution, that cat in your lap clearly displays behavior that mirrors his majestic King-of-the-Jungle ancestry.

Fortunately (for us), cats remain independent, nearly-wild creatures, keenly in touch with their inner nature. They make no apologies for this either. If catdom had a rallying cry, it very well might be: "This is who I am. Take it or leave it."

In part, it's that very "attitude" that makes us adore them so.

By living with us, though, the felines we adore have had to make some adjustments. Sort of a trade-off with side-effects. Sharing our lives brings with it certain Kitty indignities; not being able to hunt freely or being relegated to using a litter box, to name only two. So, perhaps to salvage their independence, our calculating cats have made sure that they train us! You could say we cat owners live by the "claw" of the land.

Kahlua and Cream are typical examples. These two strays were adopted by a northern California woman. In their household, windows eventually became a big issue. To open them or not to open them, that was the question.

Naturally, Kahlua and Cream love the windows open wide – as up close and personal to real nature as they'll get. Most of the time, this presented no problem for their owner, who gladly thrust open the windows each morning. But when winter set in, and it got cold and damp, she preferred the windows closed.

So they hit upon a compromise...sort of. Now, on cool California mornings, the owner sits wrapped in a blanket (shivering, I might add), while both cats are happily poised on the sill – in front of wide-open windows! (Can't you visualize their smug Cheshire Cat grins?)

Mitzi's owner is another example. Each morning, Mitzi jumps onto her owner's head to wake her. Does Mitzi's human companion lock her out of the bedroom? *Noooooo*. Does Mitzi ever get punished? *Nooooo*. (Truth be told, the majority of cat lovers don't believe in punishment.)

The solution they came up with? No contest. Mitzi won. Now her owner sleeps with two pillows over her head – so Mitzi can keep jumping to her heart's content. (Of course, if you want to keep your cat from walking all over you, you could try sleeping...standing up!)

This charming tale of author Charles Dickens and his candle-snuffing cat gives a clear picture of just how quickly cats can train their owners.

Dickens was writing by candlelight while his pet cat sat nearby on the table. Suddenly the candle flickered out. Dickens put down his pen, paused to pet the cat, relit the candle and then continued writing his manuscript.

A few moments later, the candle flickered out again. Again Dickens put down his pen, petted the cat and relit the candle. Dickens had barely written another sentence when the candle sputtered out for the third time. By now, Dickens was on automatic pilot, and repeated the process once more: Pet the cat, relight the candle.

Believe it or not, it took a few more rounds of this routine before it finally occurred to Dickens that it was the cat who was snuffing out the flame. You see, the cat had quickly learned (probably way back in round one) that if he snuffed out the candle, Dickens would make a fuss over him.

Smart, and obviously persistent, cats can also get around almost all of our attempts to limit their independence. For example, those paw prints that are all over your "off-limits" kitchen counter when you get home.

Most cat owners I know readily admit to being "cat slaves." Fortunately, all the love and attention we lavish on them does allow them to live longer, happier, healthier lives. But even though they are natural companions and have adapted extremely well to sharing their lives with us, our modern-day cats are still isolated from their natural world.

Yet, I've often thought that one of the most curious quirks in their relationships with us is their need for affection.

Curious, because this need for attention does not seem to exist among cats in the wild.

We're not talking here of routine stroking, ear-scratching or petting either (all natural throwbacks to the momma cat). We're talking about persistent cries to be held and caressed, squeezed and slobbered over. I firmly believe that our cats have reserved these cravings only for us.

And, oh, the strategies cats can come up with for getting us to obey! Sometimes their demands for affection know no bounds.

My Little Guy, for instance, is so insistent on being fussed over daily that he makes a continual nuisance of himself. When he decides he wants to be held, he jumps in front of my feet, cuts me off at the pass, slides to a stop just in front of me, and gazes up with a "Well?-What-about-it?" expression. He keeps up this routine, following me everywhere, until I give in and pick him up.

Other cats get downright cranky when they want affection. Delco always waits outside his owner's bedroom for his early morning cuddle. In a rush one morning, Delco's owner happened to bypass her without the usual dose of hugs.

Delco was not too happy. To make his point, Delco wrapped his four little legs around his owner's legs and

15

clung on for dear life – while his owner kept walking. Delco wouldn't let go until his owner stooped to lavish him with the affection he felt (knew) he deserved.

If you've ever wondered whether cats are capable of love, perhaps this tale will put an end to the question.

Shorty's human family included an 18-year-old who was about to leave home to start her freshman year in college. During all the years they had been together, the teenager was definitely Shorty's favorite in the household (and vice versa). Of course, Shorty had no idea her buddy was about to leave home.

The girl kept a collection of stuffed animals in a pile by her bed. For the past few years, they had remained untouched by everyone else in the family, including Shorty.

Right after the daughter left home, the stuffed animals – one by one – began appearing in various places around the house. First, a favorite teddy bear turned up in the kitchen. Then a Ninja turtle moved downstairs to the family room. Eventually the daughter's favorite, the Cookie Monster, wound up in the living room. Every day, the mom would return each stuffed animal to its rightful place in her daughter's room, but they continued to show up around the house.

The thefts only stopped when the coed returned home from college for vacation. And they always began again immediately after she left.

Owners who leave their cats for long periods of time often wind up creating lots of lonely Kitties. Far too many people think of their cat as an object that falls somewhere between a piece of furniture and a wind-up toy. They assume that because cats are so independent, they really don't need our company.

Nothing could be further from the truth.

Oh, sure, many cats do just fine thank-you-very-much being alone...for a little while. But most would rather have human companionship, and have actually come to depend on having us around. Besides, there's a pretty big difference between being alone and being lonely. There's no question that Kitty enjoys a catnip toy or a window perch with a view to distract her. Even better is you!

It is true that in the wild cats are usually solitary creatures, seemingly seeking out other cats just for mating. But cats show a remarkable need for attention from other cats. Anyone with a multi-cat household knows how true this is.

Being left alone can result in nerve-wracking boredom for a cat – and, ultimately, in the sort of loneliness that can create a crazy Kitty. Your cat may show signs of unhappiness by grooming herself excessively. She might even chew her tail to shreds. It's not unusual for lonely cats to express psychosomatic illnesses, too. (That's certainly one way to get your attention.) They're not faking it, though; they really can be ill. The illness simply is brought about by emotional problems triggered by loneliness.

Some folks think a turned-on TV provides a good substitute for spending quality time with Kitty. Take my advice: Save the electricity! A group of animal psychologists in Germany studied the effects of TV on pets and found that too much TV actually can make your cat crazy. It seems a cat who "watches" TV more than an hour a day becomes nervous and suffers severe loss of appetite.

Make no mistake about it: Even if your cat doesn't actively seek companionship, she still prefers having someone around. (After all, there still are those food cans to pry open!) In fact, cats who receive enough attention and companionship will be gentler and more docile. That's why two cats are better than one.

It is difficult for cats who are used to living only with humans to become part of a multi-cat household. And it's especially touchy each time you introduce a new cat into the existing population.

Some cats manage to take over the running of their own multi-cat environments themselves.

Rhubarb, for example, is a Maine Coon cat and one of eight felines in the household. He rules with an iron paw, and is generally tolerant of the rest of his roommates. But if there's ever a dispute among the other cats, Rhubarb first determines exactly who started it, then ends the argument with a whack!

More often, though, the job of managing multiple cats will fall to you. There are some things you can do to help lessen the pain of their adjustment – particularly for the cat who's having to accept a newcomer.

Always keep the new cat

separate for a few days – or even a week – preferably in a room by herself with the door closed. This helps the older cat get adjusted to the smells and presence of the new cat. It's also important that you don't displace the cat-in-residence from any of her favorite places.

Above all, never decrease the amount of affection and attention that you've already been doling out to your regular cat. During this period of adjustment, in fact, it might be a good idea to give her an extra dose of TLC.

When you finally let them meet face to face, expect lots of hissing and posturing and challenges – by both cats. Then step aside, and let them set their own ground rules. They eventually will.

If things look really tough, try rubbing butter on the new Kitty before the up-close and personal introduction. Hopefully, the cat-in-residence will lick it off, thus bridging an important gap. This trick is often used when trying to get an orphaned kitten "adopted" by a new kitty mom.

Then ... pray.

Getting cats to accept each other isn't always simple. Maybe that's why they don't often show signs of grieving for, or missing, another cat either. Personally, I've never observed my cats even noticing the absence of one or another of their housemates. Yet I do recall watching a very touching sequence on a TV nature documentary about wild mountain lions. An eight-month-old male cub had been attacked and killed. His mother grieved loudly for him every day for months.

The reaction of the mother mountain lion may have only been instinct. But her melancholy cries for the absent cub – in the same high-pitched tone with which she had called him every day of his brief life – were heart-wrenching nonetheless.

Cats' inborn independence is often the reason people think they don't mind being alone. No one doubts that cats live by their own rules (they know perfectly well what's good for them). They aren't self-centered or selfish, but rather self-reliant, dignified and resourceful.

But cats won't stoop to follow our orders in exchange for a mere pat on the head, so there's a tendency to view them as arrogant.

Actually, I think cats cling to their freedom and independence for a darn good reason. They have a high degree of intelligence, more than just instinct. They are intelligent and inventive. Even cats who have lived cooped up among humans don't lose their essential "animalness." And usually they can survive the elements – and predators – if for some reason they're separated from their homes.

Cats must adapt. And they do. If they don't quickly find another home, they probably will become "feral." Pampered and domesticated as they may be today, they know they are just a whisker away from scratching out a living for themselves. So they straddle the domestic/wild fence in order to easily adjust, just in case conditions ever force them to go back to life in the wild.

I recently saw behavior in Red that confirms this notion.

Red has a habit after eating of carefully going around all the other cats' dishes and pawing the floor as if he wants to bury their leftovers. I had always assumed that Red did this because he didn't like the particular varieties of the other cats' food, and was giving me his "restaurant review."

In the wild, however, big cats such as cougars have a similar habit that is actually critical to survival. They bury their leftovers to make sure that the food supply will remain safe from predators – and can be eaten later when it's more convenient. It suddenly occurred to me that's exactly what Red is instinctively doing.

As I observed Red further over time, I noticed that he also wouldn't munch the remains of his "buried" meals until I got home. Once I returned, he knew for sure that his food supply would be topped off by me.

Ancestral genes, indeed!

Another side-effect for cats who share their lives with us is their dependence on us. It's generally believed that most cats seem more attached to a place than to a person, but it's been my experience that, whenever I've been away for extended periods of time, my cats kill me with kindness when I return.

There's not a whole lot of scientific evidence that points to cats pining for people – certainly not in the way dogs do. Still, I'd bet the ranch that there's some strong connection at work here. When TC, my docile white cat, was so critically ill that he was hospitalized for weeks, we visited him every day. The vet said he practically could measure TC's physical improvement immediately after each of our visits. Our presence lifted TC's spirits – and boosted his will to live.

A cat named Devon was rescued after enduring a freezing New England winter. He and his rescuer have since became constant companions. When she went off on a three-week trip, it was the longest she and Devon had ever been apart. Her husband stayed behind with the cat. Whenever he played back her messages on the telephone answering machine, Devon came tearing into the room, meowing pitifully at the sound of her voice and frantically looking around for her.

Similarly, a young woman recently moved from the west coast to the east coast. To give herself time to get settled in and to spare her cat Freddie a cross-country drive, she left Freddie back home with her significant other. It was the first time in Freddie's two-year-old life that he had been separated from his human "Mom."

After she had been gone just over two weeks, she sent her boyfriend a brand new photograph of herself. He hung it on the wall. As soon as Freddie noticed the photo, he hopped up on the back of the sofa to get a closer look. The boyfriend took the picture off the wall to show it to him. Freddie got right up to it, sniffed it and peered around the back. Perhaps this was Freddie's typical curiosity about a new object in the house, but we cat lovers prefer to think that Freddie was trying to figure out where the rest of his beloved owner was.

My cat Blueberry is as devoted a sidekick as I could wish for. When my husband's travel schedule frequently left me alone at home for weeks at a time, Blueberry provided warm and cuddly company. All during the periods of my husband's absences, even when she could freely go outdoors to roam and play, Blueberry would stay beside me 24 hours a day. Who knows why? Frankly, who even cares? It's precisely this sort of behavior that keeps them in our hearts.

In my opinion, women are among the most devoted cat lovers. Men, of course, love them too, but they don't seem to get quite as loony about them as women do. This gender-preference thing about cats actually may be rooted in our own ancestry. In prehistoric times, male food-gatherers survived by hunting in groups. Perhaps even today, men instinctively identify more readily with the group hunters – dogs – than with the solitary hunter – the cat.

Also, most women probably spend more time nurturing their cats than men do. So it appears that cats respond more to women. Of course, this isn't so. Cats are completely gender-neutral. In our household, two of our Kitties prefer my husband. They only come to me if my husband isn't around.

So if cats love us so much, why then do they always seem to make a beeline for the one person in a room who hates cats? Remember that cats actually consider us other cats, giant ones for sure, but cats nonetheless.

To our cats, we're really alpha-males (or females) in a multi-species pack. By nature, cats (and most other animal species, in fact) are programmed to be intimidated by the stares of their enemies. So when a cat enters a room full of people, what she really sees is a room full of other cats, except that they're all larger and louder than she is.

All these person-cats now begin staring at Kitty, thinking how beautiful and graceful she is. All this staring makes Kitty very uncomfortable. Then she spies the only person-cat in the room who's not staring at her – the cat hater. The cat-hater, meanwhile, keeps still and silently hopes Kitty will ignore her and approach someone else.

But all Kitty knows is that she's feeling intimidated by all those other person-cat stares, so she seeks out a safe lap. Guess who? The only one in the room not moving, not waving paw-hands, not meowing and not staring at her is the cat-hater, the least intimidating person-cat in the room. Kitty makes a beeline right for her.

So here's a hint for cat-haters (well, they probably aren't reading this book, but if you know one, you can pass along the tip): When you're in a room with a cat, make eye contact and pretend you like her!

In the meantime, we cat lovers will go on being cat lovers, enjoying the living arrangements we've established with our Kitties. But even if your cat is "an only cat," rather than only one of a bunch, all sorts of things can bring about their quirky peculiarities.

Some cats imitate humans. Blinky, a silver tabby, has learned to eat artichokes just the way his owner does – one leaf at a time, scraping off only the tasty pulp. (I don't know many humans who accomplish this as gracefully!)

Gizmo, a female tortoiseshell, has actually learned to share an ice cream cone with her owner. They actually take turns licking the cone! "Sharing" isn't an especially feline trait. (Even among the wild Big Cats of Africa, only lions keep company in prides, for example.)

But to Gizmo, her owner is just another litter-mate slightly higher up the hierarchical ladder, so Gizmo naturally waits her turn dutifully instead of gobbling up the ice cream all up herself.

On occasion, cats even might mimic other animals. For instance, Tabitha, a female cat, was raised with a puppy – and lifts her leg to urinate just like a male dog!

But cats don't learn just by imitation. They think and adjust to changing circumstances and, of course, they learn by trial and error. Come to think of it, that's what cats prefer. And it may even be a good idea to let your indoor cats hunt for their food. It helps them keep their senses sharpened. By this, I don't mean to suggest not feeding them, but I learned quite by accident by observing my cat Pepper that she didn't seem to mind at all scouting around for a meal.

For instance, Pepper's keen sense of smell – along with a never-ending appetite – set her on a non-stop mission to search out her own food. On doctor's orders, she was supposed to eat only twice a day, so I stored the supply of dry cat food in a hard-to-get-at cabinet above and to the right of the refrigerator.

This didn't stop Pepper. After weeks of persistent effort, she eventually figured out how to maneuver the cabinet doors open, contorting her body like an acrobat.

Once Pepper learned the "trick," I had to install kid-locks on the cabinet doors to stop her! Despite this obstacle, Pepper kept up her search for between-meal snacks for years.

Some cats take this you-cat/me-cat business to the extreme. Granola is a tabby who got the notion into her head that her human owner wanted "grand-kittens." No one paid much mind to Granola when she was born. In fact, her own Kitty mom had abandoned her. So Granola didn't have a chance to pick up any helpful Kitty clues about how to be a good mother.

When Granola herself became pregnant and was about to give birth, she sought out her human companions. She meowed constantly and paced back and forth until her owner followed her upstairs, where Granola busily staked out her birthing spot.

When her owner went downstairs to tell the rest of the family that Granola was about to become a mom, Granola suddenly appeared in the family room alongside her. "She came flying down the stairs after me," her owner recalled. "In the middle of her labor, no less!"

Granola meowed miserably until her owner followed her back upstairs again. This kept up the entire time Granola was giving birth. If her owner so much as stepped out of the room, Granola would leap to her feet to follow her. Only when her owner returned would Granola proceed with birthing, and eventually she had five

babies. It would be quite a few days before Granola would stay alone with her kittens without her owner alongside her. (Who says it's easy being a grandma?)

There are a whole lot of cat "doings" that could only have developed because of our cats' interactions with us. It is interesting, for example, that even though cats originally came from the desert and never laid eyes on a fish, they have the reputation for being nuts about fish.

Eighteenth-century naturalist Gilbert White thought their love for fish was nothing short of going against Nature. He wrote about this irony in *A Natural History of Selbourne*: They have a "...violent fondness of fish which appears to be their most favorite food, yet nature...seems to have planted in them an appetite that, unassisted, they know not how to gratify."

Indeed, even today, except for snatching the odd goldfish from an unguarded fish tank now and then, it's still the rare cat that will hunt for its own fish in the wild. (There is one fish-hunting feline species that lives in India. But more about that later.)

The cats' connection with fish seems to have peaked during World War II. At that time, when most foods were precious and carefully rationed, fish was an easily acquired and relatively cheap source of protein. Pet food manufacturers decided it would be a great substitute for expensive and hard-to-get meat.

Here, however, was the problem: How do you sell the public on the idea? Advertisers created the association between cats and fish. Apparently, cats also believed the ads because today, cats and fish are practically synonymous.

Regardless of how much your Kitty flips for fish, for total health, she must eat meat. She is a carnivore, after all.

Other behaviors resulting from their interactions with humans are a bit more humorous. For instance, try as I might, I still can't come up with a reason why all cats love to observe us while we're on the john. (Maybe it's just the best place to enjoy a lap.)

I think our cats call this sort of stuff "helping." We, of course, recognize it as "interrupting." Have you ever tried working with a cat on your head? They seem to be everywhere at once, on the countertop when you're cooking, on the books you're reading, and I won't even mention how they get involved in your knitting!

When it comes to the human influence on cats, even the "wilds" of suburbia can be too much for some of them. When we moved to Florida, it was the first time any of my brood had ever laid eyes on a swimming pool, and each one was destined for an unexpected encounter with it. It was just a matter of time. Eventually, each cat learned what pools are about – the hard way!

In rapid succession, and only as a result of a series of mishaps, miscalculations and misadventures, each cat at one time or another landed in the pool. Amazingly, every one of them – once they got over their fright – turned out to be a fabulous swimmer. Not a single one liked it, of course... and none ever fell in twice!

Val, bless his regal heart, was so flabbergasted when he landed in the pool that he practically walked across the water to get out. I'm sure he was more embarrassed than scared. On exiting the pool, he recovered his dignity and poise immediately, shook off the water, and strutted – head high – into the house. Val's reaction spoke for most cats who never let on that they're embarrassed: "Never let 'em see you sweat," seems to be their motto.

Which reminds me...one of the most grueling humiliations endured by some cats surely is the B-A-T-H. Owners often ponder the should-I-shouldn't-I-bathe question. If any cat I've ever known had anything to say about it, the answer definitely would be "no."

They're not nuts about this water business in the first place, and probably feel downright insulted that you even think they can't handle the job of grooming themselves on their own – a job nature has endowed them perfectly well for, thank-you-very-much.

By all means, do so if your cat is so dirty that there's no choice (like if she's gotten into the crank case oil!), or if the treatment of a disease requires it. Otherwise, don't bother.

Personally, I've never even tried to bathe any of mine, but if you feel you must, use only a mild kitten shampoo and always do it in a well-heated room, in a tub of lukewarm water (about 86 degrees Fahrenheit). Be gentle and never scare her by running water on her or spraying her with it. Scoop the water over her, never wet her head, and rub her dry with a pre-warmed towel. Some cats don't object to a hairdryer, though mine can't even stand the sound of one when I use it on myself!

A final note about bathing: No amount of sweet talk will convince your cat that this is in her best interest.

Of course, as an honest journalist, I must give at least

29

a passing mention to the many cat owners who report that their Kitties adore jumping into the shower with them. One cat, Turnip, even loves to have her own bath drawn, so she can stand in the tub up to her little ankles in water.

Getting back to the subject of cats and people, those of us who live with them can tell a whole lot of stories! If room permitted in this book, for instance, there might be a whole topic called "Look What the Cat Dragged In!"

...Or Out. Take Percival, for example, a sleek black cat with yellow eyes, who dragged his owner's sexy black brassiere from a lingerie drawer. Percival proudly trailed the bra right into the middle of the living room at the precise moment his owner's blind date had stepped through the door! At least Percival was considerate enough to be color-coordinated.

Caesar, a Siamese sock-hunter in a multi-cat household, has a favorite blue sock. He chases it and sleeps with it and keeps it – come dinner time – neatly draped over the shared food bowl...as if it were his contribution to the dinner. Whenever Caesar's owner removes the sock from the food dish, as she often does, Caesar fetches it and brings it back. If the owner forgets to remove the sock, the other cats simply eat around it.

Moonshine has two telephone habits that practically caused his owner to be disinherited from his family. Not only does Moonshine regularly lift the telephone receiver just enough to get a dial tone, but he also bats the receiver off the cradle whenever the telephone rings. When the mother of Moonshine's owner telephoned her son, she knew the call had been answered because "someone" (and you know who that is) obviously had picked up the receiver.

But nobody responded to her voice, and she was greeted only by silence on the other end. When she'd hang up and immediately redial her son's number, her next attempt was met by a busy signal (because Moonshine, of course, couldn't replace the receiver!). She was convinced that her son had purposely left the phone off the hook and insisted that he was avoiding her calls. It wasn't until she finally witnessed Moonshine's "games" herself that she restored her son into her good graces – and into her will.

Pancake is teaching her owners a thing or two, even in her old age. At 20, Pancake is arthritic, blind, slow and very, very tired. Without a doubt, she just wants to be left alone – in quiet and calm surroundings. If only...

But Pancake's household now includes Goldie, a big, restless, energetic two-year-old golden retriever. One Sunday, all the family members were sitting around the living room, enjoying a peaceful afternoon. Suddenly, Goldie decided it was time to play. She raced around the house, barking, jumping and slobbering. All five family members began "barking" at the barking Goldie, screaming and yelling at her to calm down. The noise level was deafening, and getting worse.

At this point, Pancake, who had been resting on the living room rug, opened her blind eyes, lifted her head slowly and let go the most incredibly loud, incredibly ticked-off "meeeoooowwww" the family had ever heard. The dog immediately shut up, hit the floor and didn't utter a peep the rest of the day. Neither did any of the family members.

People/cat relationships can spawn some mighty funny images. Waldo absolutely refuses to get into the tub. But the minute his owner slips into the tub to take his own bath, Waldo zooms in – and sits on his owner's head.

If a picture speaks a thousand words, I'm not sure I could do justice to a wonderful old black and white *Daily News* photo I once saw. The antique snapshot said all there was to say about the noble cat.

Picture a busy midtown Manhattan avenue. A white-gloved policeman holds a whistle to his mouth with one hand, the other outstretched to keep five lanes of Model-T traffic at a standstill. Crowds of people are gathered at the curb, staring. In the bottom foreground of the photo, a mother cat with her balled-up kitten dangling from her mouth, makes her way slowly across the busy street. (And who says New Yorkers don't have a heart?)

And should you ever doubt the high regard with which cats are held everywhere, here's a tidbit from the tiny town of Guffey, CO., population: 25. Guffey has gone and elected itself a cat as the mayor! (This is the truth, I'm not kidding.) Wiffy La Gone, an abandoned tabby, got the whole town's vote of confidence in the early 1990s. (By the way, Wiffy is female, so let's hear it for Kitty lib.) Wiffy's office is in the Guffy General store where, among the mayoral duties she performs, she catches the occasional mouse.

Some cats elect themselves to high office. Like the "deli" cat who decided he's boss of not just the west side New York City delicatessen he lives in, but also of the entire block. Admittedly, it's a tough neighborhood, but the "deli" cat is up to the challenge.

My friend Anne was out walking her dog, Mr. Ying, a Pekingese. (The Pekingese is a pretty tough breed itself, bred specifically to guard the palaces of kings.) Mr. Ying is no coward. Nevertheless, he was no match for the "deli" cat.

Anyway, Mr. Ying and his owner passed by the front door of the delicatessen. In the blink of an eye, the "deli" cat ran out onto the sidewalk and clipped the poor dog before he even knew what hit him. (Very embarrassing!) Mr. Ying suffered only minor injuries from the unprovoked mugging, but he did have a very bruised ego indeed.

Sharing our lives with cats often means sharing other things as well. Like the furniture (that's another story). I even went so far as to choose the house we live in because it was "purr-fect" for my guys. It has a huge, breezy screened-in patio for safety under the sun. Plus, a handy parade of lizards to keep their hunting skills in top shape.

Hmm. Maybe cats knew exactly what they were doing when they decided to move in with humans five million years ago!

OH, THOSE CRAZY CATS!

"A cat is like a puzzle with no solution."

–Anne Campbell

So what's up with these noble felines who snub their sensitive noses at the fabulous food we provide, then take a drink of toilet water?

And how do these kitties get all their kooky quirks and adorable antics in the first place?

We'll never know the answers for sure. But that doesn't diminish our cat-watching pleasure a bit.

Sometimes their quirks are simple – just a part of who they are, just like we humans have our many peculiarities.

My cat, Kitten, for example, adores being outside on the screened-in patio. When the weather is pleasant, I leave the sliding-glass door off the kitchen open so she can come and go onto the patio as she pleases.

Regardless of how many times in a given day she goes out there (I'd say about a billion), she always pauses at the threshold first, gathers herself up, and then tosses herself off the doorsill like a high-diver off a springboard. She becomes a blurry gray missile.

What I find so funny about her behavior is that she does it, without fail, every time she crosses the threshold. I suspect that this timid little cat finds something scary about the threshold itself. But I'll be darned if I can figure out what that might be.

After nine years, I still smile every time I watch Blueberry perform her daily morning ritual – it's like some clip from a Richard Simmons exercise video. Like clockwork, Blueberry trails after me into the bathroom, then leaps up onto the my reed-covered vanity stool. Once she has balanced herself on top of its woven seat, she then hangs over the edge – practically upside down, like a bird. She then begins nibbling off pieces of the reeds, one by one, from its underside.

She's managed to dispose of practically all the outer-edge weaving this way. What she doesn't realize, of course, is that the seat is attached now by, literally, threads. I just know that one morning it's all going to give way, and Blueberry is going to fall right through the chair frame.

Mother Nature was definitely on a roll when she created the cat. It's not news to us cat lovers that these fabulous felines have the cutest peculiarities. Their never-ending antics and endearing quirks can be so weird that you'd swear they are performing just to get us to sit up and take notice.

I love watching my cats munch their favorite snacks – peanuts, popcorn and pretzels. Red and Little Guy both insist on sharing my donuts, powdered sugar coating and all. And what about all those tricks they reserve specifically for waking us up in the morning?

Some antics, though, aren't so funny. My friend Sharon is convinced that her beloved cat, Yankee, purposely pooped right on her husband's dinner plate because Yankee knew there was a divorce in the works. Yankee never really liked the guy much, Sharon says, and figures Yankee simply was expressing his dislike for the soon-to-be-ex-hubby. Maybe it was Yankee's idea of "serving" Kitty divorce papers!

In Yankee's case, at least according to the husband, the cat was around too much. At other times, though, cats seem to evaporate into the air. It's downright uncanny, not to mention frustrating! It's as if they can run away without ever leaving home.

Who among us hasn't searched the house from top to bottom for a "missing" Kitty, then found her either in the very last place we thought to look, or else she turned up in the most obvious spot – like the first place we looked. Except we didn't see her there when we looked the first time. Now, there she sits, with a self-satisfied grin, as if to say: "Gee, why are you so surprised to find me here?" It's one of the most peculiar characteristics of cat ownership.

One cat observer says his cats vanish into "cat-space," a dimension we mere mortals cannot enter. On rare occasions, he actually has watched his cat in the act of disappearing into cat-space, he says. That's how he discovered what he calls his cat's "cat-space gateways."

One day, he witnessed his cat disappearing under a flap of cloth on the bottom edge of an upholstered chair. Aha! A cat-space gateway. He knew it was a gateway because, he says, when he immediately lifted the flap on the chair, the cat was gone! The cat had already passed through the gateway and disappeared to a place where no human can follow!

Don't bother trying to call or woo your cats back from cat-space either. She will stay in cat-space for as long as she pleases. Occasionally, shaking a can of Kitty treats might work. But the operative word here is "might." Just don't act surprised when she suddenly and magically reappears. They are, after all, magical!

Don't you also love your own cat's concept of becoming invisible? You know the drill: her head-under-the-bed-with-only-the-tail-sticking-out position.

My cats also have an uncanny knack for camouflaging themselves against furniture, or at least lounging on furniture whose color seems to flatter their own coat color. (They're so vain, aren't they?) Blueberry, the calico, snuggles on earth-tone print backgrounds. Red seeks out anything orange. TC, an all-white cat, always found the white eyelet comforter the most comforting. And Kitten, my dark gray Kitty, snoozes on a black chair.

While there are exceptions to every rule, I have my own theories about cats and color. The temperament of black or gray cats is frequently self-assured, relaxed and calm, while white cats often are more fearful and nervous.

A nocturnal creature benefits most from having a darker coat (they have less chance of being noticed by either predators or prey). Light cats, on the other hand, are more vulnerable. Somehow, cats seem to know what they look like. It would be an interesting subject to explore.

Whole books could be written just on the subject of cats and their food fetishes. Here's some of what you might find in my version of *The Feline Menu Guide:*

The most unusual appetite probably belonged to a cat owned by Mrs. Lorraine Ford. *Cat World* magazine in 1985 reported that her cat not only ate grapes, but would neatly spit the pits into a pile! This same cat also ate garlic cheese, chili con carne, pasta, baked beans, corn kernels, mashed potatoes, hard-boiled eggs, yogurt and honey, cakes and ice pops. I wonder if this Kitty ever saved room for regular cat chow?

Chessie, a Persian female, loves turnips. Koko goes nuts for peanut butter. And Charlie, a princely domestic short hair named for the Prince of Wales, loves Oreos (and, yes, he does lick off the cream first, just like you and I do).

Streaky loves cheese; but not just any cheese – she's strictly a Lite-Line-fat-free-sharp-cheddar-cheese Kitty. And single slices only, please. All Streaky's owner has to do is utter the word "cheese," and Streaky races right to the fridge.

One cat I've known and loved used to eat cantaloupe and sweet corn. One of mine eats taco chips while another begs for orange sherbet. One cat even pleads for pineapple. And a cat named Sushi eats, well...here's her story:

The chef at a Japanese restaurant in Arizona was pretty surprised when my friend Nancy marched in unexpectedly, along with her three dinner guests. It's no wonder the chef was shocked.

Nancy was supposed to be having dinner at home. The chef knew that because, only an hour earlier, Nancy had left his restaurant carrying out a huge platter of (very expensive) sushi which he had prepared for her to serve to her dinner guests. When Nancy picked up the platter at the restaurant, it had 50 plump pieces of the Oriental delicacies on them.

What the chef didn't know was that, within half an hour of placing the platter onto her kitchen counter at home, Nancy discovered only three pieces remaining. Her guests hadn't even arrived yet. In case you're wondering, Sushi was not invited to join Nancy and her friends later at the restaurant.

Here's a tale of a cat who gave back more than she took. Maggie the Cat ate an entire watermelon – then promptly died. Not surprisingly, Maggie's owners were stunned as well as grief stricken. They had no idea that cats ate fruit, much less would be capable of downing a whole watermelon. Well, they buried poor little Maggie out back, and held a proper feline funeral for her.

Over that winter, Maggie's owners were mostly snowbound and hardly went outside. When spring came, they headed out to Maggie's grave and were shocked once again. Imagine their surprise when there, precisely over the spot where Maggie was buried, a watermelon patch had sprung up!

Of course, there are healthier things in Nature's bounty to which cats often help themselves. Plants are among the things they love to nibble away at – and they'll do this indoors as a substitute for eating grass outdoors. This is perfectly natural behavior. Believe it or not, to your cat, eating grass is the same as taking medication. I guess you could call it their holistic method of inducing vomiting. What I can't figure out, though, is why they decide to do their purging only on expensive rugs, especially Oriental rugs. I'm still researching this one.

Anyway, the actual reason cats need to regurgitate is so they can rid their digestive system of painful hairballs that accumulate from their constant grooming. Your Kitty can't very well stick a paw down her own throat to do the job, so she instinctively seeks out the grasses or plants.

Since they'll eat almost anything green, it is important that they don't have access to plants that are toxic. Below you'll find the names of toxic plants and trees, and the effects they have on your pet. In most cases, if your pet has eaten any of these plants or trees, its stomach must be pumped.

Almond – difficult breathing;
Amaryllis – vomiting
Apricot pits – stupor
Buckthorn – vomiting
Caladium – swelling
Calla lily – immediate nausea
Daffodil – diarrhea
Dieffenbachia – salivation
Elephant's ear – immediate nausea

English holly – abdominal pain
English ivy – immediate nausea
Foxglove – abdominal pain
Garden sorrel – vomiting
Glory lily – vomiting
Holly – salivation
Honeysuckle – possible nerve involvement
Horse chestnut – abdominal pain, diarrhea,
    immediate nausea
Jack-in-the-pulpit – immediate nausea
Jerusalem cherry – abdominal pain
Lily of the valley – pupil dilation
Mock orange – vomiting
Mistletoe – irregular heartbeat
Oleander – immediate nausea
Peach pits – coma
Philodendron – salivation
Poinsettia – possible kidney involvement
Privet – delayed vomiting
Rhubarb – diarrhea
Skunk cabbage – immediate nausea
Wisteria – salivation
Yew – vomiting

If seeing your cat throwing up so often upsets you,
relax. The whole process bothers her about as much as
yawning bothers you.

Sometimes it isn't what they eat that drives you nuts,
but what they won't eat. They're about as finicky as all
get out. Morris the Cat once shared this bit of advice
with his fellow felines: "The cat who doesn't act finicky

soon loses control of his owner." Indeed, the word "cat" might just as easily be spelled f-i-n-i-c-k-y.

They have quite a list of what they want. They like to eat fresh food – a little bit at a time and at frequent intervals. They really are nature's nibblers, preferring small amounts many times a day. Considering the size of the average mouse, miniature meals are indeed the order of the day. The average mass-produced can of cat meal is equal to five mice, for example.

Cats also prefer to dine from clean bowls and in a place that's free from noise, strong light or the hustle and bustle of household activity. They like to devour "prey" in privacy.

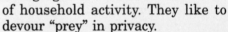
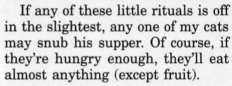

If any of these little rituals is off in the slightest, any one of my cats may snub his supper. Of course, if they're hungry enough, they'll eat almost anything (except fruit).

My own multi-cat household is often turned into a personal quality-control test-kitchen. With four cats, I can vouch firsthand to their finickiness. It's a rare meal when they'll all accept the same variety cat food! And when they look at me, as if to say, "Where's the beef?" I'm tempted to remind them that, hey, I didn't invent this stuff, guys.

Even though I have no doubt whatsoever that my cats basically see me as a walking can opener, I do get a little bit ticked off when Little Guy nips at my ankles if he thinks I'm not delivering his food to him fast enough. Some nerve, wouldn't you say? (Yet, I have to admit, there's always something about their haughtiness that makes me keep wanting to apologize to them.)

If a cat continually avoids food, there could be several reasons. If she's an outdoor cat, she might be getting her food elsewhere. (It took years before I discovered that my cat Pepper had adopted a second set of cat-feeding foster parents down the street.)

If your cat isn't eating, it also might indicate that she is experiencing discomfort in her mouth or teeth (check to see if she's excessively pawing or rubbing her mouth and face. It may mean she has a toothache or bad gums).

Stress or depression also will affect her appetite. Even leaving food out too long or serving it too cold will cause her to lose interest. If you store cat food in the fridge, try heating it slightly before serving it to her. (Can you think of any better use for a microwave?)

Maddening as their finickiness is, it may actually be biologically built in.

Cat behaviorist Desmond Morris notes that cats actually prefer lots of variety, and suggests the reason for this is adaptive. That is, a cat's ability to enjoy many different "flavors" or types of food is Nature's way of ensuring their survival.

If one kind of food supply were to dwindle, for instance, they always can switch to a new food or another source of food. Unlike your cats, not all animals in nature are programmed to do this, and that's why species can eventually die out. Studies have actually shown that when cats are given a choice between a routine food or a new food, they will more readily choose the new variety.

Doesn't "finicky" seem a whole lot less finicky now that you know it really is flexibility?

You also might have noticed that cats appear finicky –

pardon, flexible – about the water they drink, like the toilet-bowl water I mentioned earlier, for instance.

It shouldn't be at all surprising that they enjoy drinking from the bowl. While it surely wouldn't be my preference (nor yours, I assume), this habit is perfectly understandable. Water in the toilet bowl is always cold. The bowl becomes the Kitty equivalent of a gourmet water bar.

What I do get a kick out of, though, is observing my cats making their decision between drinking from the regular Kitty water bowl (which I freshen every day) or heading for the john. Of all my cats, Red prefers cold water the most, so without fail he winds up in the bathroom. But watching his decision making brings up images in my mind of wild lions in the plains of Africa.

Red always goes first to the water bowl in the kitchen and takes a sip. If the water isn't cold enough for him, he leisurely wanders ever-so-slowly through the house, down the hallway and eventually makes his way to the bathroom for an ice-cold drink. Admittedly, this is no vision from a *National Geographic* video but, for me at least, it illustrates the wild-animal-at-the-water-hole concept.

A calico named Bridget is so devoted to this toilet-bowl thing that, should the bathroom be occupied when she's thirsty, she'll patiently wait outside the door until her owner vacates the premises.

Dim-Sum has a whole other *modus operandi* when it comes to water. Before he lowers himself to take a sip from his water bowl, Dim-Sum always pushes the water dish around first so the surface of the water is moving.

Another cat, Chloe, insists that her owners leave a faucet dripping so she can lap at leisure. If they forget to set the drip for her before leaving for work, Chloe meows loudly to remind them.

Some cats can be quite clever about how they get their water. My friend Anne was cat-sitting for her neighbor's cat, Jack. Jack, it seems, has a fondness for drinking water only from a running faucet. Every time Jack wanted water, he'd lead Anne to the sink so she could turn it on for him, and then Jack would leap onto the sink to drink.

When her neighbor returned to claim his cat, Anne mentioned how cute Jack's habit was and how eagerly he'd jump up for his drink. "Jump?" asked the neighbor, stunned. "But Jack can't jump." Oh yes he can. He simply preferred not to jump and had trained his owner to lift him up to the sink to drink. Jack had his owner wrapped around his little paw for years, but when his owner was gone, Jack was smart enough to know he'd have to make it up onto the sink on his own!

Besides their fussiness about food and drink, cats also have an amazing repertoire of quirky habits. Take those places they seek out for comfort. In one friend's household, the pilot light of a gas kitchen stove provides a toasty surface between the burners. On especially cold days, it's not unusual to see all of her six grown cats piled onto this space, huddled together.

In my house, Little Guy has staked out a deep decorative pasta bowl on the sideboard in which to burrow down. All curled up, this pale-beige cat resembles a mound of dough in the bowl. Some day, I'm going to post a note on the bowl with instructions to "knead gently and let rise overnight." (I wonder if he'll get the joke?)

We stressed-out humans may sometimes have trouble sleeping, but cats suffer no such problems. Of cats and sleep, American essayist Joseph Wood Krutch aptly wrote: "Cats are rather delicate creatures and they are subject to a good many ailments, but I never heard of one who suffered from insomnia."

Samantha obviously doesn't. She snoozes blissfully in the closet – on top of the vacuum cleaner canister. One day, her owner tried this experiment: She draped a sock over Samantha while she was snoozing then went to work. When she returned nine hours later, Samantha was still asleep on the vacuum – and the sock was still draped over her!

I once tried a similar test with my white cat TC, who used to love falling sound asleep on my office desk right in front of the telephone. One day, I inadvertently placed a magazine right on top of TC, asleep in his usual spot. When he didn't budge, I added another magazine on top of the first one. Pretty soon it became a challenge to see how much weight TC might tolerate before he'd wake up and scoot off.

To make a long story short, by the end of this experiment, TC was still snoring beneath a total of 12 magazines, a three-ring loose-leaf binder, a throw pillow, two paperback novels, a steno pad, a man's shoe, a staple gun, Scotch tape dispenser, a batch of other small office-supply items...and more. TC finally did awaken, but only because the telephone rang.

Alex has taken over two of his owners' sock drawers for sleeping accommodations. But Alex doesn't just slip into an open drawer. First, he actually pries the drawer open with his paw, then removes all the contents – and, when it's empty, jumps right in for a nap. One of Alex's owners thinks this habit is so cute that she now leaves her sock drawer ajar for him. Her husband, however, has taped his shut!

Speaking of socks (footwear, that is; not President Clinton's feline friend), the owner of one Kitty sock hunter just doesn't know what to make of his Kitty's sock-hunting raids. His cat Alcazar also manages to open the sock drawer, but when Alcazar pulls out dozens of socks, he systematically wanders around the house, depositing them everywhere. Is Alcazar trying to teach his human owners to hunt, or is he merely making a comment on foot odor?

When it comes to hunting, indoor cats need to be particularly clever. Mondo enjoys sitting on the windowsill watching birds, but he's smart enough to realize that his presence on the sill scares birds away. So one day he devised a game of "Gotcha!" – well, almost gotcha.

Mondo positioned himself on the floor in such a way that he could still see the window, but was well-hidden enough by the sill to "fool" a bird into landing. When he spotted the flitting bird outside, Mondo sprang up in surprise. Here's where the limits of Mondo's trickery did him in: The window glass stopped his attempt, and the whole game

47

— and the headache — ended up a bigger surprise to Mondo than to the bird.

Okay, so not every cat is an Einstein. But the brain power of some can be quite impressive.

Inkspot, for example, is a country cat smart enough to have a career in hunting...well, *mouse*-ing, to be exact. Inkspot was adopted specifically to keep her owner's rural house free of mice; but she wasn't permitted to roam outdoors (where presumably there'd be so many mice to feed on that Inkspot might neglect her indoor job).

When Inkspot's owner first noticed that her cat was spending an excessive amount of time in the laundry-room closet, she really didn't pay it much mind. The closet's door latch needed repair, so Inkspot could easily slip in and out. Until it was fixed, the owner figured, heck, might as well just let Inkspot enjoy her investigation.

One day, Inkspot's owner took a tall bucket from the laundry-room closet, placed it in the sink and, without looking, began to fill it. It wasn't until the bucket was half full that she noticed four mice swimming around in the water. She wondered how on earth those tiny mice managed to get into the big bucket.

Since then, whenever she uses the bucket, she finds at least two live mice inside.

Apparently, Inkspot has figured out that the tiny mice can't escape over the deep sides of the bucket and is using it to stash her rodents. Personally, I think Inkspot is a genius!

Certainly, ingenuity is a trait that most cats possess. But in the multiple-cat household, ingenuity becomes an essential survival tool. Some of the most clever behaviors I've seen happen is when one cat is trying to outwit another.

Diego and Frieda are two cats bearing the names of a real-life couple, the passionate Mexican artists Diego Rivera and Frieda Kahlo. However, Diego (the cat) is jealous of Frieda (also the cat). Whenever the owner's attention is lavished on Frieda, Diego immediately runs to the food dish and starts eating – deliberately making loud lip-smacking, chomping cat-eating noises in the process.

When Frieda hears Diego munching, she gets very excited and immediately runs into the kitchen to eat, too. She wants to make sure that Diego doesn't gobble up all her food. As soon as Diego is sure that Frieda is involved in eating (and therefore distracted), he immediately runs to his owner before Frieda realizes what happened. By the time Frieda looks up again, Diego is firmly settled in his owner's lap, purring contentedly.

One cat's ingenuity even outwitted his owner – almost! Mickey and Mouser are two cats who get along just fine, except when it comes to food. Mickey always eats Mouser's food, a habit that was distressing their owner (not to mention poor Mouser). So she finally devised a plan for feeding Mouser separately.

She placed Mouser and his food in the bathroom and then closed the door to let him dine in peace. It didn't take long for Mickey to get wise to what was going on. In order to get in on the action, Mickey began hiding in the tub just before mealtime. He'd wait patiently behind the shower curtain until his owner had left the room and closed the door behind her.

At that point Mickey would immediately leap out and eat Mouser's food. Not surprisingly, his owner soon discovered his shenanigans and quickly reversed their feeding pattern – and now feeds Mickey in the bathroom instead.

The pursuit of play seems to bring out some of the wackiest quirks in cats. Playtime, while obviously amusing to the cats doing the playing, seems even more amusing to their owners. Why else would a grown adult, such as I, agree to spend hours at a time crumpling up tiny pieces of note paper to toss to Blueberry? Or focus the beam of a flashlight on the wall so she can try to catch it?

Blueberry loves chasing a flashlight beam so much that she'll get excited if she just sees me holding the flashlight – even if I only intend to use it to find something buried at the back of my closet. When her hearing was still perfect, Blueberry would come running in from another room if she heard me "click" on the flashlight.

While I know lots of cats who like to play fetch with wads of paper, Riddler is the only cat I know who fetches plant leaves. And he actually initiates the game by picking off a leaf from a house plant himself, then bringing it to his owners to throw for him. Whether they're busy or not, they usually agree to play. On occasions when they don't, Riddler just returns again and again to the plant, returning each time with another leaf. (The leaf that Riddler fetches is non-toxic. Because the cat loves this game so much, his owners got rid of any poisonous plants.)

Well, it was a surprise to no one but Riddler that the plant eventually wound up leafless (his owners breathed a sigh of re-leaf, you might say). But a dead plant couldn't stop Riddler. He simply shifted to other items, such as small pieces of paper.

This seems a pretty lame choice for such a clever Kitty. However, it wasn't the paper per se that makes Riddler unique, it was the lengths to which he would go to acquire it. He'd tip over the garbage pail and rummage through its contents hoping to ferret out papers to bring to his owners. (Is Riddler beginning to sound like a dog to you, too?) By the time he had perfected his game, Riddler was bringing his owners the most amazing assortment of papers to throw – coupons, notebooks, even dollar bills!

Ben Hur also likes to play fetch, but he prefers those little foam-rubber golf balls you can buy in a pet shop. He jumps up onto his owner's bed and deposits one of the tiny balls at her feet. The game of toss-and-fetch then begins, and continues until Ben Hur calls it quits.

One day, the foam ball he dumped in front of his owner was soaking wet. Of course, she imagined all sorts of reasons why the ball was drenched, none of them pleasant. Shortly afterward, she spotted Ben Hur in the bathroom, staring into the toilet bowl.

He was poised in that typical cat-on-the-toilet-seat stance, ears

51

pointed forward, rear end up and tail wagging back and forth. She looked into the bowl to see what he was doing. What she found was a dozen of Ben Hur's foam balls bobbing in the water. Mind you, he wasn't just standing there watching them float. He was busily swirling the water with his paw to get them to bob around.

I think that Ben Hur is pretty amazing. His owner thought so too . . . that is, until Ben Hur began placing some pretty inappropriate items in the toilet. Here's just a partial list of what eventually wound up in the toilet bowl: rolls of toilet paper, a Tupperware storage container, socks of all sorts, even an heirloom bracelet.

Needless to say, in Ben Hur's house these days, the toilet lid is down.

If what Ben Hur did is any indication of what cats can do when their owners are around, just imagine the highjinx some cats come up with when their owners are away! Dickey's owner went off on a short business trip, and left mounds and mounds of hard food for Dickey to help himself to while he was gone. But Dickey didn't eat very much of the food at all.

Instead, over three days, Dickey carefully and methodically placed every one of the thousands of nutritious pellets around the house, in the cushions and under the couch, behind the bureau and under the rug, inside some shoes and on top of the bookcase.

When Dickey's owner came home, he spent an entire week turning his house upside down, tracking down every morsel and cleaning up Dickey's damage. Needless to say, he doesn't take too many business trips anymore.

Dickey's owner figured this behavior was Dickey's way

of saying he hated being left alone. But, in fact, I believe Dickey was actually doing what I referred to earlier regarding Red burying his food. In his owner's absence, Dickey couldn't be quite sure that anyone would come by to fill up his food bowl, so he simply hid it for protection. That way he could eat it at a later time.

Another owner came home and noticed toilet paper trailing all over the house. Naturally, she started to pick it up. By the time she followed the trail, she was all the way downstairs in the basement. Kitty had discovered where the extra supplies were kept and had unwound an entire roll.

Then there are the Kitty kleptomaniacs – thieves disguised as cats. Zsa Zsa loved to steal her owner's clothing, particularly her hair accessories. (This cat has definitely earned her name!)

Another couple's cats regularly become thieves when the couple goes out for dinner. Usually, the cats only hide toys under the beds. But one weekend, when Shatzie and Pumpkin had been alone for 72 hours, the couple returned to this scene:

The cats had brought four toys downstairs, moved three living room pillows into the kitchen, and taken a three-foot-long bolster from the daybed and dragged it into the dining room. With Shatzie and Pumpkin weighing in at only eight pounds apiece, their antics would've been quite a sight to behold.

CAT CHAT

❧ ❧ ❧ ❧ ❧ ❧ ❧ ❧

"The problem with cats is that they get the exact same look on their face whether they see a moth or an axe-murderer."

–Comedienne Paula Poundstone

Just what is it that makes a cat a cat anyway? Does some single defining trait describe them? Independent, perhaps? Or curious? Maybe psychic or courageous? How about confident, resourceful and intelligent?

My favorite is *loving*.

Surely, most cats (except maybe some purebreds) look pretty much the same. Especially the alley cat varieties. Same size. Same body characteristics. Give or take a change of color here and there, and a cat is a cat is a cat.

I'm certainly not saying this is bad in any way. In fact, this attribute of "sameness" is precisely why I adore cats. If I'm around a dog, for example – whether a stray dog, a neighbor's dog, even dogs of friends or relatives – it is perfectly obvious that each dog is different. Some hunt. Some slobber. Some bite. Some don't. And they certainly don't all have equal appeal (at least to me).

Ahh, but cats. They are another story. I can be anywhere in the world, come across a cat, and in an instant I know who he is. It doesn't matter if he's an Italian cat or a British cat. A rich man's cat or a homeless cat. With cats, there's no guesswork.

Looking into the nature of cats may help you understand them better too.

All cats are territorial, even those that live indoors. They live in family-type hierarchies according to a very carefully defined social order – and heaven help the intruder!

Inside my house, each of my cats lays claim to anything with a flat surface as his or her own – from an entire room to a corner edge of the bed. Of course, indoor cats have less space available to claim as their own territory than they might outdoors, but they can always use the third dimension – up!

Outdoors, it's especially important for cats to stake a territorial claim. It could be nothing more than a backyard; or it could be quite large – limited only by how big an area a cat feels she can defend. New cats in a neighborhood have to fight to be accepted and to win territory; and neutered females are way down the rungs of the social ladder. These are two of the main reasons I no longer allow my cats outdoors.

A cat establishes territory for the same reasons that we live in homes or apartments: She needs a safe place for sleeping, eating and playing. (Only cats don't have to pay property taxes. I knew they were lucky!)

Each cat's territory includes a few kinds of spaces. First, she needs a private place where she can sleep and feel safe. Then there are the commonly held grounds which she will share with other cats. There's also the meeting grounds where a batch of cats will meet, sort of like the local pub! There's also an outer part of her territory, where she can hunt and roam.

One way or another – usually by battling it out –

55

cats establish a clear pattern of pathways and highways among themselves. Often, they'll "time-share." That means they use the same areas but at different times. When they fail to agree on the rules, expect the caterwauling to begin.

In our household, Blueberry is usually very careful about crossing the territorial path of Little Guy. The only time there is a problem is when Blueberry needs to get into the garage to get to the litter box. Heaven help her if she encounters Little Guy somewhere along the pathway that Little Guy has staked out as his.

Cats actually use their claws to help mark territory. In the act of scratching, sweat glands between the paw pads give off a scent that's then transferred to, say, a tree trunk outdoors – or my treasured table indoors. This is how each cat begins to consider the scratched area her own.

One reason that their claws retract is so they always remain protected and sharp, partly for this purpose of establishing territory.

When Blueberry rubs her head or the side of her chin against me – or the furniture, or trees, or other cats or, for that matter, just about anything that'll stand still long enough – she's actually depositing her scent on objects she considers part of her territory. It's as if she's saying, "This is mine."

This is her way of telling the other cats that certain things are part of her territory.

To anoint me with her special scent, Blueberry uses the glands on her forehead and around her mouth and chin.

These glands produce chemicals called pheromones which she transfers by rubbing. Considering that Blueberry could have chosen to "mark" me by spraying urine, I'm doubly delighted that she rubs against me instead.

Cats "spray" to stake out the boundaries of their territory. The spray leaves a powerful scent that is easily detected by other cats – and anyone else with a nose! Experts say that cats can tell just how long ago another cat's scent was laid down and whether or not they need to pay attention to the warning it signifies.

When I lived in a northeastern suburb, my cats were indoor/outdoor cats. Back then their need to make repeated trips around their territory was more obvious then than it is now that I keep them indoors.

In those days (or rather, nights), they used to behave like a crew of watchmen on their rounds, eager to check their territories. They adored making these repetitive inspections. However, they never seemed to want to do this for very long. They'd go out and check, and then come in again.

The reason their checking was so rhythmic is due to the built-in time-clock of their scent marks. When they're outside, they rub a landmark or spray it to keep rivals away. But the staying power of this scent becomes weaker and eventually disappears.

This brings about the

need for yet another visit outside – to do it all over again. Once complete, they're ready to trot back in. To me, of course, it felt like the zillionth time they had appeared at the door.

In the wild, cats could come and go as they please. In my house, however, the door stands in my cats' way. It didn't take them too long to figure out that I was the solution to the door problem. A cat door with a flap helps. But we didn't have one, so I was it! Even though their outdoor territory these days is limited to a huge screened-in patio, they still like to make their periodic checks. And, for the record, this doorman doesn't even get tipped at Christmas!

Once cats get their territory figured out, all they have to do is figure out how to deal with each other. Author and anthropologist Elizabeth Marshall Thomas describes a cat hierarchy as a wheel. The highest-ranking cat is at the center while the others are arranged around the rim. Within this well-ordered structure, each cat measures itself against the top cat, but not necessarily against each other.

In this wheel structure, cats seem to have a keen understanding of their own relative rank. Unlike a hierarchy established, say, like the rungs of a ladder, the wheel arrangement may also play a part in reducing fighting...sometimes.

Thomas' description of hierarchy perfectly explained my multi-cat household during the 12 years when my first cat, Val, was the unequivocal top cat. Since Val was our first – and a very mature, regal, self-assured cat at that – there never was any question about who was the boss.

Val had to give the go-ahead before any new cat was accepted into the household. As even stronger evidence of his authority, he'd sit poised on the edge of our bed, head held high. From this vantage point, he'd glare at other cats standing in the bedroom doorway. They wouldn't so much as venture into the room.

In the 12 years Val ruled this household, not a single cat ever challenged him.

When Val was about nine years old, he contracted feline leukemia. Feline leukemia is highly contagious – and fatal. There was no choice but to isolate Val. Fortunately, our home enabled us to do that easily. We installed screen doors to safely separate the indoor cats from Val who lived happily for three and a half more years on the enclosed patio.

For that entire time, Val was physically apart from them, but visible – and his leadership remained unchallenged. Until Val died, that is. Most curiously, the very day Val died, every one of the other cats scrambled for the top position. Suddenly, there was a tremendous amount of infighting, hissing, disturbances and a general unsettling of the whole group.

By the time they rearranged themselves, Red became sort of a substitute or temporary Top Cat (not really dominant; sort of the top cat by default), followed by Pepper and then Blueberry.

When Little Guy eventually joined the household, he shook up the hierarchy once more... Red, now older by a few years, didn't seem to mind surrendering his top position. Today, Little Guy rules pretty much unchallenged as Top Cat.

Still, the top position has never been held as supremely unchallenged as when it was held by Val. Little Guy is basically an immature cat, so his position seems always a bit flimsy. Once in a while, Red seems to give him a run for his money. And when Kitten entered the picture, the spokes on the wheel shifted again – though Blueberry still ranks last. Actually, the whole order of things is a little bit shaky.

If there's one lesson I learned, it's to let them work it out themselves. I ignore the shenanigans of hierarchical behavior. Somehow, they all work it out themselves.

Moonie, my friend Anne's cat, is lowest on the totem pole in her household, and Poopsie, the top cat, has a real dislike of her. So Moonie, who loves to sleep alongside Anne, is often prevented from doing so by Poopsie. Moonie finally figured out that sneaking into bed when the lights are out increases her chances of successfully snuggling up next to Anne. You do what you gotta do.

In any multi-cat household, it becomes pretty obvious that cats don't bond automatically. Often, they seem to only tolerate each other. They – and I – seem happy to just avoid fights. Yet, within the framework of a multi-cat household, they all exhibit a great deal of social behavior and interaction – grooming, playing, romping, sleeping and eating together. It's part of the pleasure of living with several cats.

Of course, competition and staking out territory creates tension from time to time. Without fail, one Kitty or another will hiss or spit in order to snatch the sunny spot by the window or a more appetizing meal. In the meantime, each stakes out a favorite "owned" spot.

Even if they sometimes take a dislike to one another, like Little Guy and Blueberry, it often doesn't last too long. Just imagine a dozen territorial humans trying to live together!

Some multi-cat owners seek out behavioral psychologists for their misbehaving animals. Others try to soothe ruffled tempers with homeopathic remedies. Others just move into bigger houses!

I've chosen to let them do their own thing, provided no one gets hurt. However, there are times though, when I have to referee a fight and either distract them or separate them.

From the cat's point of view, even aggressive behavior seems justified. Often, it's just a matter of re-establishing position. After all, there can only be one Top Cat per household and sometimes that cat is challenged. (Sounds like our Presidential elections!)

Some people think that cats will get along better if they're from the same litter, the same age or the same size. It's true that Blueberry and Bucky, who were litter mates, were also really great friends. But Pepper and Blueberry – who were mother and daughter – never got along after Blueberry grew up. Despite being Blueberry's mother, Pepper may as well have been from the moon as far as a relationship between the two of them was concerned. They had no apparent love connection.

When Pepper became stone deaf, however, she was treated very differently by the other cats. Some were more patient with her, as if aware of the challenge. Others seemed to take advantage of her deafness.

What could have happened was that because she couldn't hear them, she appeared to be ignoring them – and their warnings. Maybe that ticked them off. Once in a while – and much to Pepper's unending surprise – she'd get suddenly bopped or swiped at. As far as she was concerned, their anger came out of nowhere.

To her unending credit, Pepper did remarkably well considering her deafness. Actually, her hearing loss was the last challenge in a lifetime of physical problems. She no longer could hear things like the can opener at meal times, so she began sleeping in the kitchen, right on top of the counter, so there was no chance of missing a meal.

When all my cats were allowed out, none ever stayed away longer than just a few days (unless something awful, like an accident, prevented her return).

The incredible lost-cat-returns-home stories, however, are as long as some of the journeys themselves. A cat's uncanny ability to travel enormous distances, over totally unknown territory, and to return to their homes is called *psi trailing*. For decades, psi trailing has been under serious study by Duke University's parapsychology laboratory. Still, no one quite understands exactly how cats do this.

Certainly, psi trailing demonstrates a cat's amazing physical (some say even supernatural) ability – not to mention his loyalty, devotion and love. But many experts don't agree and suggest instead that the true answer is not quite so bizarre.

A cat's homing ability may rely on a built-in navigation

system similar to that used by birds. At home, the cat subconsciously registers the angle of the sun at certain times of day. When she's taken away, she finds her way back again by using a combination of her internal biological clocks, trial and error, and that angle of the sun. She's so good at doing this that she doesn't even need a clear day to navigate properly. At the same time, she's also sensitive to the earth's magnetic fields.

So, okay, let's accept that the cat doesn't use supernatural power; and that, instead, she actually manages to find her way back home over hundreds of unfamiliar miles based only on this complicated scientific formula. Frankly, I think that's even more amazing.

A cat in rural Nevada added his own spin on the phenomenon of psi trailing. Gandolf's owner had left him in a neighbor's care while she went off on a week's vacation. When she returned, the neighbor broke the bad news that Gandolf had disappeared a day earlier. About a month later, Gandolf's owner got a call from a woman in a neighboring town. Gandolf had showed up at her house – the house he had lived in two-and-a-half years earlier. Gandolf had walked five miles in blistering 100-degree heat, braving wild coyotes and crossing the interstate, to return there.

Wouldn't you love to know why Gandolf waited more than two years before heading back to his original house? I sure would. If I wanted to guess, I could say that, when his owner left for her vacation, Gandolf waited a week for her to come home. When she didn't return, he thought his vanished owner had gone back to their previous home and high-tailed it back there to find her.

Of all the amazing abilities demonstrated by cats, psi trailing isn't even the most extraordinary. Take the nine-lives thing. It's definitely more than just the brand name of a cat food. Cats and the notion of nine lives have practically become synonymous.

While it's obviously not possible to have more than one life, cats do seem to cling more firmly to the one life they've been given. The bit about nine lives may have arisen as a result of people noticing how cats manage to survive all sorts of accidents and upsets – and still come out smiling (even if they are limping). Nine has always been a mystical number (like the Trinity of Trinities, the luckiest of numbers). It's possible that the general aura of mystery and magic that always has surrounded cats simply wound up mythologized.

Just consider the cat's "righting reflex." Imagine how wondrously weird that might have seemed to a cat owner in the Middle Ages – who had no clue to the cat's biology. Of course they would have thought it supernatural.

This miraculous bit of acrobatics actually is quite complicated, and is the result of a complex organ in the inner ear that determines a specific sequence of events.

Simplified, this organ transmits information to the brain about the position of the cat's head in relation to the ground. In fractions of seconds, the brain commands the head to change position to put it square with the ground.

When the head is level, the cat first flips the top half of her body around to face the ground, then flips the rear. In the process, she uses her tail to adjust for any overbalance. Finally, she's perfectly prepped for landing and reaches terra firma on all four feet with her back arched to cushion the impact.

The trick to success, though, is time. A cat needs a minimum of 1.8 seconds to right herself. And even though she can accomplish this in something as short as a one-foot fall, her chances of success are better at greater heights (within limits).

She reaches a "terminal velocity" of 60 mph and after righting herself, lands with her limbs spread like Superman's cape, often walking away relatively undamaged. They're the indisputable champs at landing safely – most of the time. Keep in mind that even if they land upright, they can sustain severe injuries from impact.

Experts say few cats would survive a fall of more than 60 feet (though there is a cat on record who survived a 46-story fall). My friend Anne told me that at New York City's Animal Medical Center, so many cats fall from skyscrapers that vets there have an annual lottery to compare which cat has survived the greatest fall. The winner one year had fallen 27 floors!

Some cats seem uncannily blessed with the ability to defy death to a stunning degree. One nine-lives story involves Rajah, an elegant Abyssinian who was hit by a car. His right front leg was almost detached and he was in shock. He had a broken back, suffered cardiac arrest, multiple seizures and a collapsed lung, and was now also blind. Rajah's owners were heartbroken and were told to expect the worst. The doctors were talking euthanasia. When they visited Rajah, he could barely lift his head. But several surgeries (and $3,500) later, Rajah recovered, and now can walk, run – and jump.

Their amazing stories of survival sure can give us cause for paws...er, pause.

Benson, for instance, sure was a live wire! The tiny gray tabby nearly lost all his nine lives at once. As told by Beryl Reid in her book *A Passion for Cats* (published by the Cat's Protection League), when Benson was three months old, Reid's two daughters awoke from sleep to tell her they heard funny crackling noises that seemed to be coming from under their bed. When they investigated, they found Benson lying motionless and lifeless on the floor. He had chomped his way through the electric cord on a bedside light – it was still in his mouth when they found him! And those crackly noises the girls heard actually were the sparks flying from his poor little mouth.

After 30-seconds of mouth-to-snout first aid, poor little Benson began to breathe, but the vet gave little hope for his survival. By the following morning, however, Benson not only survived but, except for a very scorched mouth, he was his perky old self in no time.

When Jinx, a black cat, arrived at the home of one Mrs. N. Laramy in Devon, England, he looked as if he already had lost a few lives. He was practically starving, covered in sores and full of ticks.

Mrs. Laramy nursed Jinx back to health, and he happily took to hanging out in the warmest spots in the house. One of his particular favorites was the front-loading washing machine. The front door of the machine was left open and unknown to Mrs. Laramy, Jinx jumped in. Unwittingly, she shut the door and began the wash cycle. During the final spin, however, she heard a constant strange knocking that she could not trace.

When the wash was finished and all the socks removed, Mrs. Laramy was shocked to discover Jinx's bedraggled lifeless body inside. She tried desperately to restore him, pumping water from his stomach and shaking him upside down. Mrs. Laramy finally brought breath to his lips with the kiss of life and a jigger of whiskey. Jinx is fully restored now... but won't go near the washing machine!

Another cat, Muffy, was smart enough to stay away from the washing machine, but not smart enough to avoid the dryer! In her book, *Cat Tales*, Sara Pitzer tells how Muffy jumped unnoticed into the dryer before her owner finished loading it. Needless to say, Muffy was a mess – her breathing labored, her whiskers crinkled, her fur singed and her paw pads scorched. But only a few days later, Muffy was well enough to return home from the vet. Pitzer adds that Muffy now is "even a little suspicious of anyone wearing clean clothes!"

This story appeared in the *Charlotte Observer*. A man tried to rescue a kitten from a pine tree by backing his pick-up truck against the tree. He then stood in the truck bed and lassoed the top of the tree. He pulled on the rope to bend the top of the tree so he could reach up to the kitten. But the rope snapped, the tree straightened and, whoosh, like a pebble in a sling shot, the kitten was catapulted over the roof of the house and into a neighbor's swimming pool. Maybe the lesson here is, let the cat come down by herself. It eventually will, you know. As one vet put it: "We've never found a dead cat in a tree."

No one quibbles with a cat's ability to predict earthquakes anymore. But one cat should have been more in touch with her own instincts. Spot was sunning herself on a window ledge of a California apartment building. Suddenly, she was shaken from her perch by an earthquake and fell 10 stories. Her only injury was a broken leg.

Jacob actually survived a sinking. One coal-black night in the winter of 1964, a Dutch ship, the Tjoba, moved cautiously down the river Rhine. Suddenly, an unexpected and violent collision left the boat so damaged that it immediately started to sink. Within minutes, it was on the river bottom. All the crew were saved, but poor Jacob, the ship's six-year-old cat, was trapped below deck and went down with the vessel.

Eight days later, when cranes raised the wreck, the crew was allowed to board to collect whatever was left of their waterlogged belongings. Imagine the captain's surprise when he opened his cabin door to find the last thing he ever expected: There was Jacob, shivering with cold and starving. To everyone's amazement, he had survived more than a week underwater in a bubble of trapped air.

Perhaps the record holder for accident-prone survivors is Sam, a Siamese belonging to Marie Clark of Buckinghamshire, England. Sam managed to be dropped, trapped, stung, nearly drowned, crushed, roasted and hanged, and then narrowly escaped being burned to death in a blaze.

As a kitten, Sam was dropped on the doorstep and got a cracked jaw. That was life number one.

He nearly lost life number two while his owners were away. Sam squeezed himself into a spot behind a brand new fireplace that had to be ripped out to release him. Life number three was snuffed out when Sam ate a bee which stung him. He had a horrible reaction that swelled his head and he couldn't eat for two weeks.

Life number four was used when he slipped inside a laundry bag just in time to be dumped into the washing machine where he met the same fate as Jinx. Life number five slipped away when Sam rummaged through some rubbish. It turned out that the rubbish was ready to be ground up and Sam was saved in the nick of time by the garbage man who heard his cries.

Sam's sixth life hinged on his being rescued from a tree, where he was hanging by his collar. Number seven burned out when his home caught fire. He was so overcome by smoke, a fireman had to revive him with the kiss of life.

But, hey, who's counting?

A CAT-A-LOGUE OF WONDERS

I t's a well known fact that animals can think and make plans. One type of Japanese monkey can make snowballs, and Koko, the "talking" gorilla, communicates with her human companions in sign language. Here's a tale that may prove cats know how to count:

A little black cat had recently given birth to kittens. She had hidden them in a rock pile near a farmhouse for safety. One day, Melinda, the young girl who lived in the farmhouse, caught sight of the little black cat, and noticed immediately that the cat had recently had kittens. Melinda followed her to see if she could discover where they were.

Naturally, the cat made a beeline for the rock pile, where Melinda spotted three teeny Kitties, two tabbies and an all-black one just like Momma cat. Melinda carefully scooped the trio out of the rock pile and hurried back to the house, cradling the kittens in her palms. She wanted to put them in the house for safekeeping, to ensure they would survive.

Of course, Momma cat seemed distraught at first. But when Melinda's family allowed the cat inside each day to feed and tend to her kittens, she didn't seem to mind (maybe she figured it was like leaving her kittens in day care). Besides, she was a farm cat, and liked having the freedom to roam.

Several weeks had passed when very early one morning, Melinda stepped out onto the front porch. There on a chair, right next to the door, were three tiny mice, neatly lined up in a row – one for each kitten. Now that's a smart Momma!

If the smarts of that little cat impress you, you might like to know that your own cat possesses an IQ that is surpassed in the animal kingdom only by monkeys and chimps.

Okay, it is true that if you consider brain size alone, maybe your cat is no superstar. But the common yardstick for measuring evolutionary development compares the ratio between brain size and the length of the spinal chord.

In other words, this indicates how much gray matter (or brain, in other words) controls how much body. This is where your Kitty comes in higher than any other domestic animal.

We already know that cats think and adapt to changing circumstances, and that they learn by observation, imitation, and by trial and error. If Mom's a hunter, for instance, chances are pretty good that her offspring will be too. (Interestingly, kittens learn more quickly from their own mothers than from examples set by cats that are not related.)

Cats can imitate humans too. My entire brood, for instance, has learned that the knob opens the door. They can't manage to open it themselves, of course, but they definitely make the connection (however vague) that touching the knob opens the door. Whenever they want to go out, they lead me to the door and then stare at the knob or try to tug at it.

 Evidence from lab experiments indicates that cats possess a high level of intelligence. At Wesleyan University, Dr. Donald Adams has shown that cats can remember successful problem-solving strategies. They then use that insight to think their way out of difficult or unusual situations.

This is defined as "learning to learn," something we humans strive to do at college. Not that anyone is saying your cat is Harvard material, but they have been shown to exhibit greater problem-solving ability than dogs. Tests conducted by the University of Michigan and the Department of Animal Behavior at the American Museum of Natural History concluded that while canine recall lasted no more than five minutes, cats' recall lasted as long as 16 hours – exceeding even that of monkeys and orangutans.

Considering that cats evolved as desert animals – in climates that were dry, dry, dry – it isn't so surprising that they aren't nuts about water. There just wasn't a whole lot of water around! Certain breeds do seem to like water more than others do, however. Abyssinians have been known to enjoy joining their owners in the shower. The Van cat, rare outside its native Turkey, loves to swim. And Turkish angoras and Manxes savor a splash or two.

But the most unique may be a wild cat known as "the fishing cat." She actually swims in order to catch fish. She's called the Bengali Mach-Bagral, and Nature gave her extra-long claws which she uses like fish hooks for spearing her prey. This fishing cat is found in Nepal, Burma, Southern China and parts of India.

Because of their desert origins, cats have adapted incredibly well to life without water. Their kidneys can excrete toxins without requiring a lot of fluid, for instance.

Generally, the average healthy cat needs very little fluid to maintain her health. Some research has even shown that cats fed a steady diet of canned cat food – which is 70 percent water – may not even choose to drink additional water. (Still, fresh water should always be available for them.)

To me, it has always seemed a puzzle that the same cat who hates cold food always and without fail flies out of the woodwork at the sound of the fridge door opening. Oh, well, that's a cat for you. The reason they find cold food unappealing is because they are predators. In Nature, cats would consume their prey fresh – at warm body temperatures. So I serve their food at room temperature, or give their leftovers a quick zap in the microwave.

If you listen carefully to what your cat says, you'll notice that she has the ability to make 17 different sounds.

According to a study done in 1944 by Mildred Moelk, who researched cat vocalization, cats use nine consonants, five vowels, two diphthongs – and one triphthong (I'll bet they can't say those words, though). In terms of the number and difficulty of the sounds they make, some scientists place cats right up there close to us humans. Of course, the most common sound that cats make is "meow" which, given their egos, probably means "me."

Writer Katherine Briggs has observed that, "The most domesticated of cats somehow contrives to lead an outside life of its own." True enough. What falls to us, though, is the difficult task of trying to get them to come home when we want. Sometimes we have to find ways to get inside those hidden lives of theirs.

Here's some advice about how to get your outside Kitty to come home when you call her (provided she's in the neighborhood, of course), or to get your indoor cat to respond to your call. I must warn you ahead of time, a trained cat is an contradiction in terms.

To get your Kitty to respond to your call, first get her to associate your call with food. I know it sounds pretty low, but it works. Cut down on her early evening meal so she's feeling a little hungry by nighttime. Then rattle a box of dry food and give a quick "toot" on a whistle.

Keep rattling her box of treats until she comes. (Mind you, I'm not guaranteeing results here, and don't bother writing to me if she doesn't respond within a reasonable time. Of course, you may feel pretty dumb standing there whistling, while your cat snoozes under your bed oblivious to all this.) If she comes within a reasonable time of your whistle-blowing (and not just by coincidence), reward her with her treat and the remainder of her dinner.

Continue this routine each night until she's familiar enough with the ritual to respond just to the whistle — and always reward her for returning.

Oh, the things we do for our cats! There are cat fanatics who give coming-out parties, throw baby showers and plan birthday parties for their Kitties. But a guy in England takes the prize for throwing the biggest bash.

The millionaire owner of a 14-year-old Persian decided to throw a yacht party for his cat. The millionaire invited 150 guests, and had his cat driven to the party in a limo.

Know what? The cat slept through it all. (Are you surprised?)

At last, we may finally get a chance to sleep like our cats. No, I don't mean on the floor, curled up into a ball in a patch of sunlight with your hand across your nose (although, don't knock it, you might like it).

What I mean is that scientists at California's Scripps Research Institute have discovered a compound found in sleeping cats that may be the miracle ingredient we've all been waiting for. It's expected to bring natural drug-free sleep to millions of us insomniacs. (Terrific as it sounds, though, it all seems rather ironic to me, since most of us are insomniacs in the first place because our nocturnal cats keep waking us up all night!) Stay tuned.

Here's another batch of curious cat-related facts
Did you know...?

♪ There once was a law on the books of Reed City, MI making it illegal to own both a cat and a bird.

♪ In 1973, then-California Governor Ronald Reagan signed into law prison penalties for kicking or injuring another person's cat.

♪ On the other hand, President Dwight D. Eisenhower, a well-known cat-hater, forbade cats in the White House, and actually instructed his staff to shoot them on sight. (So how'd we ever came up with a slogan like "I Like Ike" for this guy?)

♪ A cat named Mousam received a notice to report for jury duty. When Mousam's owner notified the board of elections that their potential juror was a cat, Mousam was disqualified. Bet you'll never guess why. NOT because Mousam was a cat, but because he couldn't speak English!

♪ At last count, four museums in the world are devoted entirely to cats: One is in Basel, Switzerland, two are in the Netherlands, and a fourth in Ainvelle in northwest France. (Now those folks understand fine art!)

We ordinary folks aren't the only ones who fret about our furry friends, though. Humphrey, the Downing Street Cat, was as familiar a presence in the old prime minister's quarters as the prime minister himself. When Humphrey suddenly disappeared, it caused quite a stir in the highest ranks of London life.

According to the cat's press spokesman (yes, the cat had his own), Humphrey had not been eating too well recently, and also suffered a long-standing kidney ailment. They assumed he'd gone off somewhere to die.

Everyone loved Humphrey, and nostalgic, sentimental stories began circulating about the feisty cat – from his brave bouts with illness, to fond remembrances of his many escapades. One story people were fond of telling was when Humphrey had managed to snatch a few ducklings from the pond in St. James' Park. Another was how he raided a robin's nest in the garden of No 10. Downing St.

They were about to declare Humphrey "officially" dead (his obituary was already in the works) when, wouldn't you know it, he strolled back into Downing Street. Looking a little worse for wear, he was immediately tended to by a local vet, and, as of this writing, he's doing fine.

Here's a tale about French author Alexandre Dumas and his mind-reading cat: Dumas lived with his mother and a cat named Mysouff. Each morning, when Dumas would leave for work, Mysouff would join him part of the way, then would turn back and stroll home.

Each afternoon, Mysouff would reverse the process and meet with Dumas at the same midpoint spot and they'd walk home together. If Dumas' mother ever forgot to open the door when it was time for Mysouff to meet Dumas in the afternoon, the cat meowed and scratched until she did.

This wasn't the most unusual part. More curious was the fact that, on days when Dumas decided not to return home at his regular time, Mysouff didn't bother leaving the house. How did the cat know that?

Indeed, their mind-reading abilities can be downright uncanny. Consider that cat carrier, for example. The carrier may only be associated with a once-yearly trip to the vet, but to my cat Red, all I have to do is think about getting it out from the garage – and he vanishes. Red also is on a daily dose of pills and manages to disappear the instant I go into the kitchen to fetch his medicine. How he knows I'm going for his pill – and not for, say, the ketchup – I'll never know.

There are thousands of stories about cats who have stepped in in the nick of time to save the lives or property of their owners, whether alerting them to fires and earthquakes or even attacking an intruder or two. Here's one:

A cat who lived in a British pub suddenly flew into a state of great anxiety. No amount of stroking by his owner seemed to help reduce the cat's agitation. He ran wildly back and forth between his mistress and the pub's fireplace, until the woman became so alarmed that she called for help. Lo and behold, a robber was found hiding in the fireplace chimney. He had planned to conceal himself there until closing-time, and then slip out to rob the place.

My friend Roberta's cat, Howie, helped nab a cat-burglar. Remember, a cat-burglar is a thief adept at coming and going without attracting attention (just like a cat). In this case, it was a case of the cat who nabbed the cat-burglar.

As Roberta's family was getting ready for bed one rainy night, they heard a muffled sound that they assumed was far-off thunder. Howie, however, was staring out the window and wouldn't stop yowling until Roberta went to the window to see what he was trying to tell her.

She saw a thief walking away from the house with her daughter's brand new 10-speed bike. Roberta called the police who rescued the bike and arrested the thief. You see, the sound that Roberta thought was thunder actually was the thief opening the garage door, and Howie was the family's alarm.

Of course, in most cases, the tables are turned, and it's the humans who rescue cats. Not all of the rescues are simple. One new home-owning couple practically tore their house apart to rescue a stranded Kitty. Though, when they started, they had no idea what an effort it would take.

The couple accidentally discovered the stray cat when they heard his loud shrieking. The sound was coming from behind their built-in microwave. Apparently, the cat had fallen in there through a roof vent. So, out came the microwave. But before they could entice him to come out, the Kitty skittered down behind the trash compactor, so out came the compactor.

The owners even tried baiting a hook with fish to lure Kitty out. It didn't work. Since they didn't welcome the thought of tearing down the house any further, they resorted to Animal Rescue. Eventually, out came the cutest

79

little gray Kitty, who now lives happily in the house he almost destroyed.

Then there are the love-conquers-all stories.

A California woman volunteers for an organization that humanely traps feral cats. Feral cats, of course, are those that remain in – or revert to – the wild. However, this organization reduces their risks of living in the wild and makes sure that the cats remain healthy.

The volunteers test the trapped cats for disease, neuter them, give them their shots, then set them free again. For the rest of their natural lives, these wandering cats have access to shelters that are set up to feed them.

One day, the volunteer trapped an adult male whom she described as a "hopeless case." He was full-grown, way beyond the age of being socialized, and she had a very difficult time trapping him.

After they did manage to catch him, he was given a clean bill of health, and the volunteer released him. After she let him out, however, he kept coming back to her house. Soon, it became apparent that he wanted to become part of her household.

He began rubbing against her legs and he even let her stroke him. Within days of his release, he let himself be picked up and brushed. He was domesticating himself! Now, he sleeps alongside his rescuer every night, and whenever he's ill he stays with her.

Even more unusual, however, are the cats who help rescue other pets in distress.

Among these amazing stories is Ernie, a cat who once saved another cat from being buried alive. An Ohio woman had lost her Kitty and was sure she'd never see him again. Shortly after, a strange little kitten appeared at her doorstep. Being the cat-lover that she is, of course she fed her and brought her inside.

Knowing first-hand how painful it is to lose a cat, she made every effort to find the kitten's owners. She even left her door open in case the kitten wanted to wander back to her home. But the kitten simply stayed and went to sleep.

That afternoon, the kitten headed for the compost pile in the garden and began screaming frantically. The woman picked up the Kitty and brought her back in, but she zipped right out and did it again. So the woman rooted around in the compost heap.

Suddenly, her hand hit upon a motionless, furry, object lodged in the space between the concrete slab and the fence. She drew out her nearly-dead, dazed and bewildered cat who had fallen in and been trapped there. Both Kitties were thrilled and they all lived happily ever after.

COOL CATS

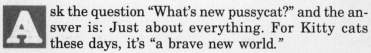

"Everything that moves serves to interest and amuse a cat."

–F. A. Paradis de Moncrif,
French writer

Ask the question "What's new pussycat?" and the answer is: Just about everything. For Kitty cats these days, it's "a brave new world."

Think about it: As we approach the year 2000, cats haven't even gotten the hang yet of coping with the invention of the automobile. And now they're having to go whisker to whisker with the Electronic Age.

Today's high-tech world must seem confusing indeed. A Kitty's environment is filled with ringing telephones and buzzing faxes and whirring camcorders. (My friend's cat Archie once accidentally filmed chirping birds on his owner's camcorder!) There are TVs and VCRs and computers, microwaves, and so much more.

To their credit, the poor little things are doing their level best to adapt. Of course, by this I don't mean that cats have become computer hackers or home-video buffs, but some seem pretty darn close. (Does anyone out there know how much damage cat hair can do to a keyboard?)

Here are some tidbits about Kitties who've discovered our 21st-century technologies, and how they're facing them head-on.

In Lancelot's case, it was feet-on. One day, while cooped up alone in his apartment, Lancelot decided to jump onto the telephone. He knocked off the receiver and by sheer coincidence happened to paw the automatic speed-dial button that was programmed to dial 911.

Naturally, the 911 dispatcher didn't get any response from the anonymous "caller." So the dispatcher was concerned that something really horrible might be taking place. She immediately dispatched the police to Lancelot's location.

When the cops showed up at the door – guns drawn, no less – the cat-culprit was already off somewhere sleeping and Lancelot's owner was assumed to be a practical joker. The police didn't find this a bit funny, and neither did Lancelot's embarrassed owner. Lancelot isn't allowed to use the phone anymore.

Other cats find computers fascinating. Fletch enjoys watching the *Star Trek* screen-saver images on his owner's computer. And Fillmore is fascinated by the mouse pointer moving across the screen. One human computer buff installed a multi-media setup for his Kitty. This guy plays animal sounds for his cats. He says the wolf and dog sounds are his cat's favorites.

One cat recognizes the sound of "goodbye" from the computer networking service America On-Line, and dashes from anywhere in the house when he hears it because it means his owner is free to pet him!

Personally, I've always considered the debate about who's better, cats or dogs, to be rather distasteful and point-less. But this cat-versus-dog controversy appears to be raging on the world-wide computer network. Here's a collection of observations shared by cat-lovers:

- ♪ Cats are dogs with a college education.
- ♪ If you call a cat and it comes running, what you have is a dog.
- ♪ Cats rule, dogs drool.
- ♪ Dogs teach you how to love. Cats teach you how to live.
- ♪ The difference between a cat and a dog is that a cat can bark...and doesn't.
- ♪ Cats are smarter than dogs. You can't get eight cats to pull a sled through snow.
- ♪ Dogs sniff, cats wink.
- ♪ When dogs leap onto your bed it's because they adore being close to you. When cats leap onto your bed it's because they adore your bed.
- ♪ Dogs bury bones, cats hide [their] thoughts.

On the more serious side, a computer chat-room actually has been a life-saver for some cats.

One woman wound up saving her new kittens' lives because of her computer on-line connection: Rosie, her two-year old Manx, decided to have her kittens at 1 a.m. Rosie's owner was home alone because her husband was working his night job. Rosie wasn't doing so well with the parenting problem on her own, and her owner didn't know what to do to help her.

She stroked Rosie repeatedly and tried to soothe her through the process. Eventually, Rosie had five kittens.

After they were born, however, Rosie's owner noticed that momma cat had neglected to chew off their cords and two of the newborns couldn't nurse. If assistance wasn't applied soon, the Kitties would surely die. So Rosie's owner signed onto her computer to ask for help.

Right there, in Cyberspace, in the middle of the night, she located two guys with veterinary training who "talked" her through the medical dilemma. The three-way conference was a huge success – all the cats survived.

Computer's aren't the only technology that has affected cats. TV's Discovery Channel seems to be a particular favorite of several Kitties.

Petunia, a cat who watches the Discovery Channel, has a favorite nature program about the big cats of Africa, particularly the hunting tactics of lions. After watching the part about the choke-hold that lions use on the throats of their victims, Petunia tried the same tactic on her owner.

Peanut, a tiny eight-month-old kitten, is thrilled by another Discovery Channel program featuring pumas. One segment shows the mother puma caring for her babies. Peanut's owners hold her up to the screen and when the baby pumas appear on the screen, Peanut extends a paw out to touch them.

At first, Peanut's owners were flabbergasted by this interaction, so they tried an experiment. They let Peanut watch other scenes, but nothing else brought a response.

Curtis the cat sings along to old movies on TNT – but only to MGM's old musicals, mind you.

Chuckles likes to watch the weather channel and hockey games so much that when her owners go away, they leave specific instructions for the pet sitter to keep the TV tuned to these programs for her. For about half an hour, Chuckles watches the hockey puck flipping back and forth. During commercials, she takes a cat nap.

A product called "Video Catnip" describes itself as an "entertainment video for cats to watch."

The 24-minute video features frisky squirrels and darting birds to keep your housebound Kitty as spellbound as if he lived in the woods.

Your cats may be no Siskel and Ebert, but the video (which can be ordered by calling 1-800-521-7898) does get rave reviews from some cats. It was developed when the producer noticed that his own cat Stick got excited watching a National Geographic TV special.

The producer says he has since learned that almost any indoor cat will instinctively react to seeing small critters parading across a TV screen. For the starring roles, he recruited every bird, squirrel and chipmunk in his home state of West Virginia to the set. Many cats, says the producer, recommend the video.

Some cats get so addicted, says the producer, that they even sit in front of a darkened TV, hoping their owners will turn on the set. Others come running when the VCR is turned on. Some Kitties meow at the TV set, others sneak a peek around back, some even lie down and roll around. Nobody eats popcorn, however.

Other videos from the company include fish, quick-darting lizards and even other cats. What next? Cats fighting with their owners for the remote?

CAT·ANATOMY

"A masterpiece."
Artist Leonardo daVinci,
referring to the cat

Leonardo should know. He created quite a few masterpieces himself. So no book about cats would be complete without a reference to their extraordinary bodies. For sheer beauty and grace, nothing comes close to the cat.

Everything about their bodies is designed for balance, secrecy and the hunt – from their padded little paws and retractable claws to their amazing flexibility.

An Indian proverb says a cat is a lion in a jungle of small bushes. For sure, cats are right up there with their jungle cousins, but cats also are portable – and you can snuggle with them in bed. I'd say that's a pretty terrific combo of wild and wonderful.

Their unique muscle structure is specifically designed for "springing" into action. Jordan, a cat named after basketball great Michael Jordan, can leap a good six feet into the air without a running start, and can jump up to the fireplace mantel in order to reach the fish tank. He's even retrieved a toy mouse that was placed on the top hinge of the front door.

But it's also a cat's collarbone – or more precisely, the lack of one – that makes her practically collapsible, and they can plunge headlong anywhere they want to with incredible accuracy. I'm always amazed how Red, for instance, manages to jump from a sitting start on the floor into the narrowest opening high on one of our bookshelves.

You also could say the "eyes" have it. Cats' faces are flat between the eyes, so both eyes are able to work together more easily. Their stereoscopic vision is a rarity in the animal world. As a result of both eyes working together, the cat focuses more accurately and sees three-dimensionally. With this ability, Red can keenly judge visual distances with uncanny accuracy.

Contrary to popular myth, though, cats cannot see in total darkness – and their daytime vision is only fair. However, they can see better than humans in semi-darkness. They also can distinguish brightness seven times better than we can.

As nocturnal hunters, their eyes are adapted to work in the dimmest light, scooping up the smallest scrap of available light. Their vision generally is blurred at the edges and they see best at six to 20 feet. But when it comes to movement, your cat doesn't miss a twitch.

(Incidentally, it's a no-no to feed dog food to your cat. A steady diet of canine chow can cause blindness. It lacks taurine, a substance crucial for your cat's sensitive eyesight.)

It once was believed that cats were color-blind, but we now know they actually can distinguish between certain color variations. Basically, they see the world around them as dull shades of blue and green. They don't, however, see red.

Even though they have this narrow spectrum of color vision, it isn't known exactly how this affects their per-

ception of the world around them (mine, it seems, mostly yawn). It appears that cats don't attach much signifi-
cance to color or pay much attention to it. In nature,
color isn't particularly necessary to a cat's survival.

Here's one of the funniest stories I've ever heard about
color: Jelico is considered queen of the snake catchers by
her owner, periodically bringing the slithery serpents into
the house.

One evening, several dinner guests had just seated themselves around the table when Jelico decided to display
her hunting ability and marched into the dining room
with a small green garden snake dangling from her
mouth.

She proceeded to play with it on the carpet, making it
curl up and slink around. Needless to say, the guests
were a bit squeamish – and also discomforted by the rep-
tile's torture, so Jelico's owner removed the grateful
snake from the house. Perplexed, Jelico continued to search
around the room for it.

Moments later, the first course was served. It was a
freshly made green-bean soup. Not the purée kind, but a
soup brimming with crisp slen-
der legumes (don't get ahead of
me here).

One of the guests brought a
spoonful of soup to his mouth, and
a long green bean hung off the
edge of his spoon. No fool Jelico,
she jumped immediately into
the guest's lap with a look that
said in no uncertain terms: "Aha!

So that's where my snake went. Would you mind returning it, please?"

Of course, vegetables aren't vipers, a lesson Jelico quickly realized.

Cats' eyes are magical for other reasons, too. Those glow-in-the-dark spheres can sure seem eerie, mystical, even downright scary when they gleam out at you from the black of night – especially since your cat is one of only very few animals that can return a human's stare.

There is a simple physiological explanation for the characteristic green or gold shine of your cat's eyes. The eyes don't actually "glow."

A membrane – called tapetum lucidum – coats the eye and acts as a reflector of light. Layers of these glittering membranes act like an efficient mirror. When your cat is in the dark, its pupils open wide and light bounces off them. This ability, along with their extraordinary sensitivity to ultraviolet rays, further enables your cat to see so well in the dark.

Hearing, though, is your cat's keenest sense. Kitty's remarkable ears each have 30 muscles that control the outer ear (by comparison, our ears have only six muscles each). This allows their ears to act like SensAround, rotating independently 180 degrees, so that Kitty can collect sounds without moving her head.

Even though your snoozing cat appears to be asleep, she's only dozing and is on automatic pilot. She remains "on watch," while those little turret-like ears lift signals out of thin air like a radar saucer. She might, after all, need to spring into action at the spur of the moment – like a nearby mouse.

A cat's ears can turn in the direction of sound 10 times faster than those of the best watchdog. (The difference though, is that your cat doesn't want the job of watch-cat...unless a predator is about to grab her pray.)

She can hear sounds up to an amazing 100,000 cycles per second which, coincidentally, just happens to be the same sound pitch made by a mouse's squeal. You can get some idea of how incredible their hearing is by comparing their noise-noticing capability to yours (which is only about one-fifth as sensitive), or to dogs (which are only one-third as acute). No wonder your screeching stereo drives the poor little thing mad!

So how good is their hearing anyway? Actually, dogs have a greater range of pitch, but your cat's hearing far exceeds a dog's when it comes to distinguishing high-pitched noises.

Cats have adapted brilliantly to hunt by lurking in ambush – listening for the tiniest sound, the smallest rustle, the teeniest squeak. Their keen hearing also lets them pinpoint the precise direction and distance of their prey. No mouse (or sock) is safe. So is it any wonder that they hear the refrigerator door opening in the downstairs kitchen...when they're upstairs...in the bedroom...under the covers...fast asleep?

Even your cat's flexible tail is adapted for skill. It contains between 14 and 28 caudal, or tail, vertebrae, linked like a string of loosely threaded beads. For these "acro-cats," the tail is an important aid in balance. It also communicates a wide range of mood signals to other cats — and to us. You're probably well aware by now of the message communicated, say, by your cat's tail-held-high greeting when you get home.

The tail's back-and-forth swishing motion indicates she's on alert, perhaps for some nearby bird. She also might fan her tail in an attempt to lure a stationary bird into flight because, great as your cat's eyesight is, she can easily lose sight of a motionless bird.

In the animal kingdom, your cat's retractable claws are her most unique feature. When she extends her legs, the paws automatically expand to an extraordinary size and the claws appear.

Also, cats are the only clawed animals that walk directly on their claws, not on their paws. It's quite an unusual attribute, and if we had to explain its uniqueness in human terms, it's something akin to you and I walking on the tips of our fingers. Getting around this way on tip-toe is called digitigrade, and is a particularly useful aid for speedy running.

Obviously, these supreme hunters need to keep their claws in tip-top condition and carefully honed. My friend named her cat Freddy Kreuger because the cat slashes everything with his long claws. Cute. And not so cute.

But contrary to what you may think, clawing furniture isn't done out of spite. It's true that one of my cats long ago staked out our wooden coffee table to manicure her nails, and another does the same on our rattan family room furniture. But this isn't done to sharpen their claws either. The act of scratching is instinctive.

What cats actually are doing when they're clawing your couch cushions is tearing off the ragged edges of the sheaths of their claws. All year long, they shed their claws naturally to expose new sharp ones beneath. And your furniture is just the right height.

Personally, I've never found a commercially bought scratching post a solution to the clawing problem. For all the good it does, it may as well be an umbrella stand! But I do find that spraying a water mister at the cat does help. Problem is, I have to be there.

Frustrating as clawing is, I have never declawed any of my cats. Claws aren't just for your cat's protection. They also are responsible for Kitty's balance and other amazing feats like climbing, stretching and running. Declawing not only physically afflicts a cat – it actually maims them – but it also psychologically anguishes them. It deprives them of their only defense and is one of their most versatile tools for survival. Claws even provide an important grooming tool.

Speaking of grooming, my cats typically spend about a third of their day grooming themselves. Considering how many hours they already devote to sleep, this grooming time roughly translates to about three hours' worth of self-pampering a day. How many of us can afford to indulge in such leisure luxury!

There are several reasons they groom themselves so often. Cats clean themselves with their saliva, which is thought to contain a detergent-like deodorizing substance for keeping their coats soft, glossy and clean. Blueberry's fur, in fact, has a perpetually pleasant scent, almost like talcum powder. It's so distinctive, I can even detect Blueberry's scent in the middle of the night and know that it's she who has crawled into bed beside me, and not some other cat.

But grooming also has other important functions: It removes dead hair and skin, tones up muscles and stimulates blood circulation.

Another important tool cats have are their rough little tongues. Depending on your own sensitivity, that sandpaper tongue may delight or disturb you. Blueberry frequently licks my eyelids and nose. And while I prefer to interpret that gesture as a sign of real affection, to her the tongue is just another survival tool.

Those little prickly bumps covering the upper surface of a cat's tongue are called papillae. They're what makes the tongue abrasive, and are a holdover from when your cat's ancestors needed to keep a low profile in the wild.

The tongue's upper surface has hundreds of these small backward-pointing papillae, constructed of virtually the same substance as our fingernails. With them, your cat can use her tongue like a comb to give herself an extra-deep cleaning, leaving no cat odor to attract predators or to warn away prey.

Her tongue not only feels like a nail file, she also uses it like one. It's designed to scrape off that last little bit of meat from bones. Of course, thanks to canned food and can openers, Blueberry no longer needs that ability, but a field cat would certainly still use its tongue to get that last nutritious morsel from a mouse.

The tongue is even highly important to newborn kittens. At birth, the tongue has a rim of spines that runs along the edge. These spines help give the hungry kitten a good grip on Mom's nipple.

In addition to their physical arsenal, cats also have a sixth sense. Not psi trailing (which lets them find their way home over long distances), but a sense that is actually midway between taste and smell. The receptor for this sense is called the Jacobson's organ. It is located in the roof of the cat's mouth, and is thought to communicate signals to the sexual center of the cat's brain.

When the Jacobson's organ is stimulated, the cat opens her mouth slightly and wrinkles her nose – a response called the "flehmen reaction." You may notice your cat making a curious grimace (which looks like a tight little smile with the front teeth covered by the upper lip).

She does this when she detects some particularly stimulating odors in the environment – usually ones that are strange to her. This grimace reaction is thought to enable chemicals to be brought into contact with the Jacobson's organ. Blueberry displays this behavior more than my other cats – probably because she's low cat on the totem pole, and needs to be especially alert in a world that seems more threatening to her than to most of my other cats.

This behavior was first described and named by a former director of the Leipzig Zoo in Germany, Dr. Karl-

Marx Schneider. For lack of an appropriate English word, the term "flehmen" (pronounced flay-men) is used. It's not a well understood sense, and we humans don't have anything like it. Poor us.

Not surprisingly, a lot about their physical make-up isn't completely understood. However, one of their oddest quirks is. I'm sure you're pretty well-acquainted with that sudden spook-induced racing from one end of the room to the other. Your cat goes nuts for no apparent reason and zips by at the speed of light.

At those moments, it sure seems as if your cat is the fastest animal in the universe. At full tilt, they're clocking an amazing 31 mph and cover about three times their own length per leap. (Incidentally, cheetahs, the fastest land animals, hit their stride at around 70 mph.)

One cat observer calls this mad dash the "frantic tarantella." Whatever name it goes by in your house, this behavior is a result of pent-up energy that suddenly overflows. Remember, our Kitties are nocturnal beings and natural hunters. The sedentary lifestyle we impose on indoor cats can drive them stir crazy. The result is this nighttime frenzy.

Because they're nocturnal hunters they definitely need their daytime rest. They even do this with style. They're downright cat-atonic, sleeping practically all day, every day – clocking in about 16 hours of sleep during each 24-hour period. That's almost twice what we humans do. These laid-back critters aren't exactly the labor force of the animal kingdom. In fact, if we slept as much as they do, we'd be working from noon-to-one instead of from nine-to-five.

So what's the deal with all that snoozing? They're the cat-nap originators. Your Kitty's sleep pattern has evolved because of her ancestors' success as a predator. The physical machinery of these natural-born hunters is designed for short bursts of energy needed for high-performance over short distances.

They don't necessarily require stamina and endurance. They're so efficient at stalking and killing their highly-nutritious prey that they've wound up with time to spare. What better time-filler than a delicious nap on a full stomach?

Most of the time they sleep very lightly, so they make up in the number of times they sleep what they lack in depth of sleep. R&R has become part of their lifestyle. But even in deep sleep, their brains are as active as when they're awake and they're still on the alert for danger. So don't try pulling your tabby's tail when she's snoozing. Her wake-up time will be split-second – and she may strike out in the process.

In the final analysis, even if biology is destiny, cats really are more than the sum of their parts. They are little souls with whom we've agreed to share our lives and our space, who remind us each day that humans aren't the only special beings on the planet.

Little Guy, for instance, insists on being picked up and caressed in my arms, sometimes for an hour at a time. When he's pressed tight against my chest – purring away – there's no doubt about it: I'm sharing a heartbeat with the furriest tranquilizer in the world.